The ISO 45001:2018 Implementation Handbook

The ISO 45001:2018 Implementation Handbook

Guidance on Building an Occupational Health and Safety Management System

Milton P. Dentch

ASQ Quality Press
Milwaukee, Wisconsin

American Society for Quality, Quality Press, Milwaukee 53203
© 2018 by ASQ
All rights reserved.

26 25 24 23 LS 8 7 6 5 4

Library of Congress Cataloging-in-Publication Data

Names: Dentch, Milton P., 1942– author.
Title: The ISO 45001:2018 implementation handbook : guidance on building an
   occupational health and safety management system / Milton P. Dentch.
Description: Milwaukee, Wisconsin : ASQ Quality Press, [2018] | Includes
   index.
Identifiers: LCCN 2018014551 | ISBN 9780873899710 (hardcover : alk. paper) | 9781636941004
   (paperback)
Subjects: LCSH: Industrial hygiene—Management—Standards.
Classification: LCC RC967 .D47 2018 | DDC 616.9/803—dc23
LC record available at https://lccn.loc.gov/2018014551

ASQ advances individual, organizational, and community excellence worldwide through learning, quality improvement, and knowledge exchange.

Bookstores, wholesalers, schools, libraries, and organizations: Quality Press books are available at quantity discounts with bulk purchases for business, trade, or educational uses. For information, please contact Quality Press at 800-248-1946, or books@asq.org.

To place orders or browse the full selection of Quality Press titles, visit our website at: http://www.asq.org/quality-press.

Quality Press
600 N. Plankinton Ave.
Milwaukee, WI 53203-2914
Email: books@asq.org

ASQ Excellence Through Quality™

Table of Contents

List of Figures and Tables

CD Contents

Preface

I started my professional career in the paper industry in the early 1960s, working for a company that manufactured pulp and paper-making machinery. As a young engineer, I traveled to paper mills all over the USA and Canada. The mills provided an engineer with excellent exposure to chemical, mechanical, and electrical engineering concepts and an understanding that paper mills and wood yards and pulping areas presented a myriad of safety hazards to the workers. High-speed rotating equipment created opportunities for employees to become entangled in the machinery; the vacuum pumps were very noisy, and there was also potential for exposure to toxic or corrosive chemicals.

During my first visit to a paper mill at the Maine-Canadian border, I recall walking through the mill during a time when the machine had experienced a major paper break. There were large holes in the floor near the machine, where the waste paper, referred to as *broke*, would be shoveled down below the paper machine for reprocessing by gigantic, sharp blades. The holes in the floor were not guarded or blocked during these times. I was alerted by my escort to stay away from the area because, with all the stacks of paper being pushed around, it was not clear where the holes were; only the experienced operators should be in those areas. I was told horror stories by the old paper makers that every few years a fatality would result when an operator would fall into the broke holes. Over time, the mills developed techniques to properly dispose of the waste paper in a much safer way.

I left the paper industry in 1969 to work as an engineer and manager for the Polaroid film and camera company. I had direct responsibility for health and safety in chemical manufacturing, specialty coatings, similar to the paper industry, and battery manufacturing. All of the areas involved moving machinery and harmful chemicals. I gained a lot of manufacturing experience in those 27 years and an appreciation for the importance of maintaining a safe workplace. After I left Polaroid, I was plant manager for several years at a coating plant, where there was also chemical manufacturing using high-speed rotating equipment.

The Occupational Safety and Health Administration (OSHA) was created in 1970 by the signing of the Williams-Steiger Act by President Nixon. I was safety engineer in one of Polaroid's plants at that time. OSHA's mission was to prevent work-related injuries, illnesses, and occupational fatalities by issuing and enforcing standards for workplace safety and health and to create a better workplace for all workers. While the high incidences of injuries in industry during the 1960s created a need for action at the federal level, OSHA presented serious concerns for companies like Polaroid. (Note: Information on OSHA is provided at https://www.osha.gov /Publications/all_about_OSHA.pdf.)

Polaroid had highly secretive processes and products, and nonemployees were not allowed access to manufacturing or research areas. Polaroid did not inform workers of the identity of chemicals in containers which were marked "X" or "Y." The workers that mixed "X" could not work in the area that used chemical "Y." Polaroid management always had a high regard for employee welfare, so, over time, the company adapted to the oversight of the federal OSHA requirements—and despite some fits and starts, Polaroid continually improved its safety performance. I was fortunate to have experienced training in a wide spectrum of workplace safety hazards linked to OSHA requirements.

While OSHA continues to be a subject of criticism for its somewhat excessive bureaucracy and oversight, I believe OSHA, since 1970, has been an important factor in the reduction of workplace injuries in the United States. The injury and ill-health statistics bear this out, although there are still too many worker injuries/ill-health issues occurring every day. I believe an organization can more efficiently address its requirements under OSHA by creating an occupational health and safety (OH&S) *management system* with certification under the International Organization for Standardization (ISO) process.

In 1998, I became an ISO-qualified auditor and consultant. In the past 20 years, I have conducted quality, environmental, and safety audits in hundreds of plants of all sizes in a wide variety of industry sectors. Observing what allowed some companies to implement a very successful OH&S system, I discovered they were not implementing a *safety program*; these companies had created a safety *management system*. The differences between a management system and a program are illustrated below.

Safety Program	Safety Management System
• Dependent on individual knowledge	• Requires management oversight
• Reactive: compliance focus	• Commits to improvement
• Inconsistent record keeping	• Formalizes record keeping
• Minimizes employee involvement	• Encourages employee involvement
• "Silo" effect among managers	• Includes staff reviews
• Difficult to monitor	• Requires internal audits
	• Commonly uses third-party audit

Starting with my very first ISO 9001 audit in 1998, I observed the company's safety issues, even though I was conducting a quality audit. I would often advise my guide during the plant tour that I would notify the company of potential safety issues during the walk-around if the client agreed. My notes would not be included in my formal audit report but would be left with the client. My offer was very rarely refused. I can recall, in some cases, particularly when doing an audit in a large chemical plant, my guide would use his cell phone to record some of the observations I would make.

When BS OHSAS 18001—Occupational Health and Safety Management—was created in 2000, I became qualified to conduct audits to that standard in plants in the United States, South America, and Eastern Europe. During the 18001 audits, I witnessed some of the ways OHSAS 18001, as a management system, could help improve the organization's safety performance. I also trained internal auditors in several large plants to audit according to the OHSAS 18001 standard.

The ISO 45001:2018 Implementation Handbook explains how an organization can use a management system to both control and improve its safety or occupational health and safety performance. In this handbook, I provide guidance in building the OH&S management system in support of the organization's operations, linking the management system to the requirements of ISO 45001:2018, to support third-party certification. Included in the text are best practices as well as common pitfalls or weaknesses I have observed in various organizations. For those organizations certified according to OHSAS 18001:2007, I highlight the changes required to upgrade to the new international standard.

The ISO 45001:2018 Implementation Handbook is formatted to describe each clause of ISO 45001:2018 in four sections:

- Correspondence with the current OHSAS 18001 standard

- The ISO requirement

- Guidance on conformance to the requirements

- Questions for internal auditors.

I paraphrased the ISO requirements to describe the essence of each requirement in straightforward terms. In the guidance section, where applicable, I organized each clause as a process with inputs and outputs and provided examples of how the clause requirements can be satisfied. A CD included with this handbook contains internal auditor check sheets that can be used to assess conformance to ISO 45001:2018.

The ISO 45001:2018 standard follows the requirements of Annex SL. The International Organization for Standardization created Annex SL, which is intended to harmonize all ISO management systems' terminology and formatting. It was designed to make it easier for organizations to build their documentation when they have to comply with more than one management system standard. ISO 9001:2015 and ISO 14001:2015 were released using Annex SL formatting. After assisting more than a dozen clients in upgrading ISO 9001 and ISO 14001 to the 2015 requirements— which includes utilizing the structure of Annex SL—I observed some confusion generated by this universal formatting. While the goal of creating a common structure for all ISO standards is certainly noteworthy, some of the terminology embraced by Annex SL is not helpful, in my opinion, especially in relation to providing and maintaining documentation. The handbook outlines my concerns with Annex SL terminology and provides recommendations on how organizations can comply with Annex SL while avoiding its confusing aspects.

I wrote the ISO 45001:2018 implementation handbook with four goals:

- Provide guidance to organizations seeking certification to ISO 45001:2018

- Assist currently certified OHSAS 18001:2007 organizations in upgrading to ISO 45001:2018, while improving their present OH&S management system

- Provide guidance for internal auditors

- Provide guidance on interpretation of ISO 45001:2018 requirements.

Chapter 11 of this handbook provides a checklist for self-certification to guide organizations wishing to benefit from conforming to ISO 45001:2018 without having to seek third-party certification.

Chapter 12 provides guidance in facilitating interpretation of the new OH&S management system requirements.

Note: The contents of ISO 45001:2018 have been paraphrased in this book. Paraphrased text, by its nature, can introduce differences in understanding and interpretation. This book should be used in conjunction with ISO 45001:2018 *Occupational Health and Safety Management Systems—Requirements with Guidance for Use*. The interpretations and paraphrasing of ISO 45001:2018 in this handbook are not authorized by ASQ, ANSI, or the ISO.

1

OHSAS 18001 History and Chronology

Back in the late 1980s and early 1990s, organizations worldwide recognized the need to control and improve health and safety performance and to do so with occupational health and safety management systems. The timing of this recognition was somewhat aligned with the formation of the European Union and the establishment of the international standard for quality management in 1987.

With leadership from the British Standards Institution (BSI), the United Kingdom's national standards body, the Occupational Health and Safety Assessment Series (OHSAS) Project Group was formed and included representation from many countries. The group published the OHSAS 18000 series in 1999. The series consisted of two specifications: 18001 provided requirements for an occupational health and safety management system, and 18002 supplied implementation guidelines. The specification outlined the prerequisites for any occupational health and safety management system which would assist an institution in controlling risks and reducing accidents.

The International Organization for Standardization (ISO) did not consider OHSAS 18001:1999 an official ISO standard and did not authorize third-party certification audits. Many organizations around the world recognized the value of a certifiable safety management system and pushed for the establishment of an ISO standard. Companies in the United States were somewhat ambivalent about the need for a safety standard because they felt Occupational Safety and Health Administration (OSHA) regulations were sufficient. Many US companies, however, elected to use OHSAS 18001:1999 to improve their safety performance. By 2005, approximately 16,000 organizations in more than 80 countries were using the OHSAS 18001 specification.

BS OHSAS 18001:2007, released in July 2007, made improvements to OHSAS 18001:1999 by making it more robust and by introducing skill requirements and improving compatibility with other management system standards such as ISO 9001 and ISO 14001. BS OHSAS 18001:2007 was consistent with ISO management systems but was not under the umbrella of the ISO certification schemes. The BSI provided third-party certificates for organizations fulfilling the requirements of BS OHSAS 18001:2007. By 2009 more than 54,000 OHSAS certificates had been issued in 116 countries. By 2017, more than 90,000 companies have been certified to the BS OHSAS 18001:2007 standard.

In 2013, the ISO initiated actions to create an International Standard for Occupational Health & Safety Management Systems and chartered the ISO Project Committee (PC) 283 to develop the new ISO standard, ISO 45001 *Occupational Health and Safety Management Systems—Requirements with Guidance for Use*. This standard will replace BS OHSAS 18001:2007 and will have a certification process similar to those of ISO 9001:2015 and ISO 14001:2015 management system standards. The initial draft international standard (DIS 45001) was issued in December 2015 and followed by the final draft (FDIS 45001) in September 2017. The standard ISO 45001:2018 was released as of March 2018.

2

ISO 45001:2018 Changes from BS OHSAS 18001:2007

Organizations currently certified to OHSAS BS 18001:2007 will need to address the new (or expanded) requirements of ISO 45001:2018 with the following general groupings:

- Understanding the context of the organization and expectations of interested parties

- The integration of the occupational health and safety (OH&S) management system requirements into the organization's business processes

- Increased worker involvement and participation

- Actions to address risks and opportunities

- Planning to achieve OH&S objectives

- Expanded top management commitment

- Expanded operational planning and control requirements in relation to multiemployer workplaces, hierarchy of controls, management of change, outsourcing, and procurement, and contractors

- Revised documentation terminology

CONTEXT AND INTERESTED PARTIES

The previous OHSAS 18001:2007 standard required organizations to define the "scope"—the activities, processes, and buildings and property within their occupational health and safety management system. The new clauses of ISO 45001:2018, *Understanding the organization and its context* and *Understanding the needs and expectations of interested parties*, challenge organizations to analyze the impact of these regulations from a more holistic, proactive vantage point. These requirements are consistent with the harmonized formats established by Annex SL for all ISO management systems and implemented in ISO 9001:2015 and ISO 14001:2015. The Annex A.4.1 to ISO 45001 provides guidance as follows:

A.4.1 Understanding the organization and its context

An understanding of the context of an organization is necesary to establish, implement, maintain, and continually improve its OH&S management system. Internal and external issues can be positive or negative and include conditions, characteristics, or changing circumstances that can affect the OH&S management system.

Annex A.4.1 lists dozens of *external issues*, such as the cultural, social, political, legal, financial, technological, economic, natural surroundings, and market competition, whether international, national, regional, or local; introduction of new competitors, contractors,subcontractors, suppliers, partners, providers, new technologies, new laws, and the emergence of new occupations; new knowledge on products and their effect on health and safety.

Annex A.4.1 also lists *internal issues* such as governance, organizational structure, roles, and accountabilities; policies, objectives, and the strategies that are in place to achieve them; the capabilities, understood in terms of resources, knowledge, and competence (e.g., capital, time, human resources, processes, systems, and technologies); information systems, information flows, and decision-making processes (both formal and informal); introduction of new products, materials, services, tools, software, premises, and equipment; and relationships with, as well as perceptions and values of, workers.

To assist organizations with understanding the needs and expectations of interested parties, Annex A.4.2 provides some examples of *interested parties*. In addition to workers, interested parties can include legal and regulatory authorities; parent organizations; suppliers, contractors, and subcontractors; workers' representatives; workers' organizations; owners, shareholders, clients, visitors, local communities, and neighbors of the organization, and the general public.

Many of the above examples are intended to apply to all ISO management systems, including quality and environmental, so they are generic. There is also some overlap with internal/external issues and expectations of interested parties. An external or internal issue may result from an interested party; an example would be a legal safety-driven external issue mandated by an interested party, such as OSHA.

The majority of manufacturing organizations will have a similar list of external, internal issues, and interested parties. To highlight the concept, I have outlined the context for a chemical manufacturing company which has many challenges and hazards in its OH&S. The possible external/internal issues and interested parties related to chemical manufacturing are as follows:

External Issues	Internal Issues	Interested Parties
• Worker protection regulations • Technology related to worker safety	• New material, products • New processes, equipment • Worker representatives • Worker language • Worker capabilities	• Regulatory agencies • Industry sectors • Customers • Workers • Neighbors • Community

Chapter 4 in this handbook provides examples of several different types of manufacturing companies addressing the context and the interested parties related to their OH&S management system.

INTEGRATION OF THE OH&S INTO THE BUSINESS

Many companies, currently OHSAS 18001–certified, have integrated the OH&S into their business planning and strategy. I have audited companies of all sizes where the safety performance metrics are woven into the business plan; the key performance indicators (KPIs) assigned to quality, environmental, and business parameters also include the safety metrics of accidents and safety incidents and "near-misses." "Best-in-class" organizations have established a business management system (BMS), incorporating their financial, quality, and environmental systems into a cohesive operational model, with *safety* often appearing as the first agenda item. Chapter 9 in this handbook describes techniques illustrating the integration of the OH&S with the organization's business.

INCREASED WORKER INVOLVEMENT AND PARTICIPATION

The OHSAS 18001:2007 standard included worker involvement in hazard identification, risk assessments, and determination of controls; appropriate involvement in incident investigation; involvement in the development and review of OH&S policies and objectives; consultation where there were any changes that affected the OH&S.

When I conducted third-party audits with respect to OHSAS 18001:2007, related to worker involvement, the audited organization would usually assign an hourly representative for me to interview. I would question the individual on how he or she was consulted on OH&S issues, such as hazard and risk analysis and incident investigation, and whether the workers' inputs were considered when making changes to work areas. In some organizations, the representative was from a safety committee or a worker union.

ISO 45001:2018 increases the importance of worker involvement, making worker participation a key building block in achieving the overarching goal of reduced work-related injuries and worker ill health. Those organizations with excellent worker participation in their OHSAS 18001 system will most likely satisfy ISO 45001:2018 requirements. Other OHSAS 18001–certified organizations with minimal worker involvement programs will need to demonstrate more evidence of worker participation to satisfy ISO 45001:2018.

In my experience, the successful organizations have created a workplace *culture* where worker safety has a high ranking in the company's priorities. Chapter 10 in this handbook describes some of the techniques I have observed from organizations having a strong worker participation culture.

ACTIONS TO ADDRESS RISKS AND OPPORTUNITIES

The risk analysis requirement in ISO 45001:2018 is part of the standardization of all ISO management systems as required by Annex SL. Risk analysis was central to OHSAS 18001:2007 as part of clause 4.3.1 ("Hazard Identification, Risk Assessment and Determining Controls"). The new requirement 6.1 ("Actions to Address *Risks* and Opportunities") adds another layer of risk analysis to the OH&S management system and focuses on risks related to achieving the organization's objectives and results. I believe the risk analysis requirements in ISO 9001:2015 and ISO

14001:2015 standards are a valuable addition to those standards and can also be successfully used to enhance the OH&S management system.

The quality tool, failure mode effect analysis (FMEA), can be applied to OH&S's required risk analysis. Chapter 6 in this handbook describes this requirement in more detail with examples of application to the OH&S management system. This handbook completely reformats clause 6.1 to make the requirements more clear and removes cross-referencing of requirements and over-indexing.

ISO 45001:2018 (and all new standards) does not have a requirement for "preventive action." The idea is that the entire OH&S management system is preventive in nature, and the risk analysis approach is also preventive.

PLANNING TO ACHIEVE OH&S OBJECTIVES

ISO 45001:2018 clause 6.2.2 ("Planning to Achieve OH&S Objectives") requires the organization to define and document:

- The methods/techniques that will be used to accomplish the objectives

- The resources required

- The responsible person(s)

- Objective completion date

- How the results will be evaluated, including indicators for monitoring

- How the actions to achieve OH&S objectives will be integrated into the organization's business processes

In past revisions of OHSAS 18001, organizations would not always provide a formal plan to manage the implementation of their OH&S objectives. Third-party auditors will now expect the organization to have a defined program describing how each OH&S objective will be achieved. This requirement is consistent with ISO 14001:2015 for environmental objectives programs and should reduce auditing inconsistencies and enhance OH&S improvements.

TOP MANAGEMENT COMMITMENT

While OHSAS 18001:2007 requires a commitment from management to support the OH&S management system, ISO 45001:2018 amplifies this commitment. ISO 45001:2018 emphasizes that top management's responsibilities involve more than *delegating*. Requirements for top management are more specific with regard to demonstrating leadership and commitment. The handbook describes the approach top management can take to demonstrate leadership and commitment to the organization's OH&S management system (MS).

EXPANDED OPERATIONAL PLANNING AND CONTROL

Clause 8.1 of ISO 45001:2018 ("Operational Planning and Controls") adds several new subclauses: Management of Change, Procurement, Construction, and

Outsourcing. The requirements of these subclauses were essentially included in OHSAS 18001:2007 under clause 4.3.1 ("Hazards and Risks"), with the possible exception of procurement, or purchasing.

A comprehensive OH&S management system, when addressing the organization's hazards and risks, will consider how *changes* in the organization processes, equipment, or personnel can affect safety performance. When the organization installs new equipment or machinery, the hazards and attendant risks should be clearly identified. In a similar fashion, construction activities or contractors coming on site to do maintenance or to install machinery can create high risks to the organization.

When an organization has employees from another organization working on the premises, their safety (and the impact on the organization's workers) has to be addressed. For example, if a company outsources making chemicals or ink to another company with employees working in a section of the organization's plant, there could be situations created by the other company's workers that could impact the health and safety of the workers of the parent organization. This situation, along with other factors related to clause 8, is addressed in Chapter 8.

The clearer requirement in ISO 45001:2018, covering procurement or purchasing, is a good addition in my opinion. In the past, an experienced third-party OHSAS 18001 auditor would review the process to bring chemicals onto the site referenced to safety data sheets (SDS) to ensure the proper communications take place to instruct workers on the safe handling of the new chemical in order to avoid dangerous exposure. Procurement of items, such as laboratory devices or machinery, should be reviewed for worker safety prior to receipt by the organization.

DOCUMENTATION

ISO 45001:2018 clause 7.5.2 ("Creating and Updating Documented Information") is more prescriptive than OHSAS 18001:2007. The organization is now required to define how the organization formats their documented information. Procedures, work instructions, and forms need to include a title, date, author, reference number, and format type (software version, graphics) and whether the medium is paper or electronic.

Chapter 7 provides guidance on how organizations can create and maintain an effective documentation system in conformance with ISO 45001:2018.

3

The Occupational Health and Safety Management System as a Process

The internationally recognized standard for OH&S management, ISO 45001:2018, is built on the plan-do-check-act (PDCA) approach (Figure 3.1), the operating principle of all ISO management system standards.

In the context of OH&S management, the PDCA approach works as follows:

- *Plan:* Establish the scope, context, and policy of the OH&S. Define the hazards and risks in the workplace that have the potential to result in work-related injuries and ill health to workers. Define the legal and other requirements promulgated to protect workers from injury and ill health. Establish programs to improve the performance of the OH&S management system.

- *Do:* Implement the OH&S management system action plans and controls with input and participation by the workers.

- *Check:* Monitor and measure the processes and controls and evaluate and report the results in terms of whether the measures are reducing worker injuries and ill health.

- *Act:* Take actions to improve the OH&S management system performance on an ongoing basis, making adjustments as indicated by the checks.

While establishing the plans and actions to support an OH&S management system, it is helpful to view the OH&S as a *process* with two desired outputs: compliance with applicable legal regulations and maintenance of a safe workplace. The organization's management provides the inputs to the OH&S process: the scope of activities, the context (or business model), and the OH&S policy.

Figure 3.2 represents the core processes of an OH&S management system and is the starting point for building the OH&S management system. The next step is to define the business model for the organization with linkage to related ISO 45001:2018 requirements.

The chart in Table 3.1 can be used to connect the clauses of ISO 45001 directly to the plan-do-check-act terminology

The major clauses of 4, Context; 5, Leadership; 6, Planning; 7, Support; 8, Operation; 9, Performance Evaluation; and 10, Improvement are common to all ISO management systems as required by Annex SL. The groupings are built around the quality management system ISO 9001. The clause-numbering protocol does not fit all of the ISO 45001:2018 clauses accurately. Clause 5.4 ("Consultation and Participation of Workers") needs to be under the *leadership* of management, but, to produce the intended improvements in workplace safety, the workers need to

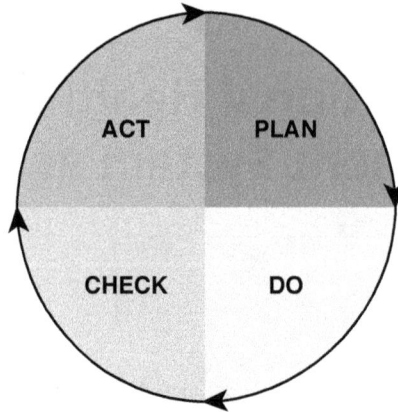

Figure 3.1   Plan-do-check-act cycle.

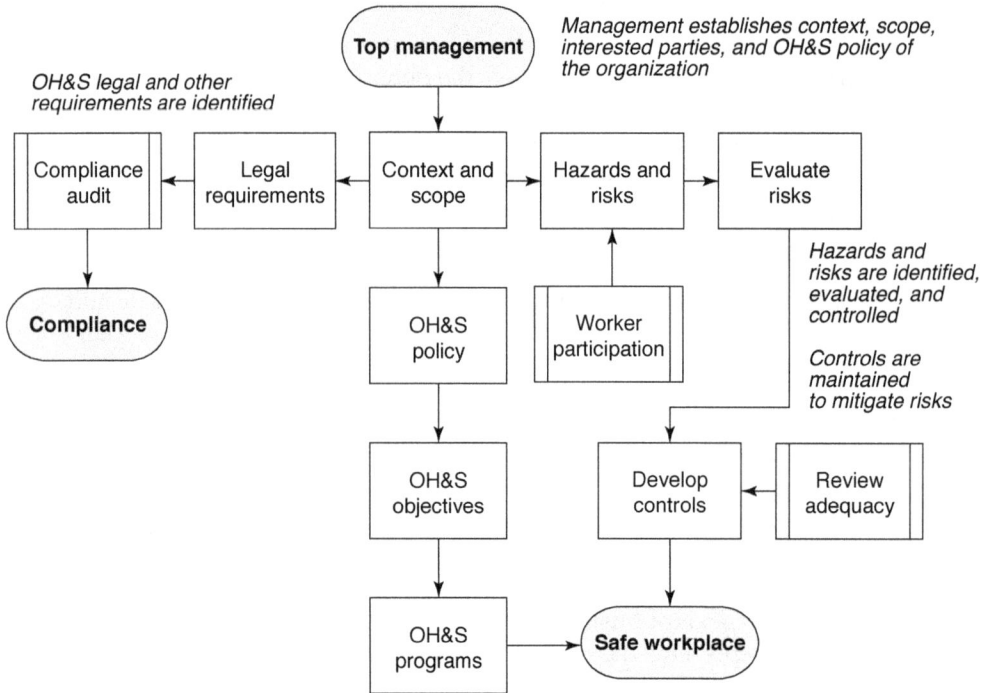

Support processes: Documentation, emergency planning, training, internal audit, incident investigation, corrective action, management review, and improvement.

Figure 3.2   The occupational health and safety management system as a process.

fully participate in the OH&S while *doing* their jobs. Additionally, while clause 8.2 ("Emergency Preparedness and Response") is part of the organization's operation, a key component of emergency response is the preparedness or *planning* processes.

For organizations looking to certify an OH&S management system for the first time, I recommend a review of what is already in place in the business, related to the core OH&S processes, before attempting to conform to the ISO requirements.

Table 3.1 PDCA linked to ISO 45001 clauses.

Plan			
4 Context of the Organization	**5 Leadership**	**6 Planning**	**7 Support**
4.1 Understanding the organization and its context	5.1 Leadership and commitment	6.1 Actions to address risks and opportunities	7.1 Resources
4.2 Understanding needs and expectations of workers and other interested parties	5.2 OH&S policy	6.1.2 Hazard identification and assessment of risks and opportunities	7.2 Competence
4.3 Determining the scope of the OH&S management system	5.3 Organizational roles, responsibilities, and authorities	6.1.3 Determination of legal requirements and other requirements	7.3 Awareness
4.4 Developing OH&S management system	5.4 Consultation and participation of workers	6.1.4 Planning action	7.4 Communication
		6.2 Setting objectives and planning to achieve them	7.5 Documented information
		8.2 Emergency **preparedness** and response	

Do	Check	Act
		Nonconformity identification and corrective action
8 Operation	**9 Performance evaluation**	
8.1 Operational planning and control	9.1 Monitoring, measurement, analysis, and evaluation	Continual improvement
8.1.2 Eliminating hazards and reducing OH&S risks	9.1.2 Evaluation of compliance	
8.1.3 Management of change	9.2 Internal audit	
8.1.4 Procurement	9.3 Management review	
8.2 Emergency preparedness and response		
5.4 Consultation and participation of workers		

Unfortunately, there is quite a bit of "ISO speak" in all international standards due to the need to cover worldwide organizations of various sizes and complexities with a multitude of languages and interpretations. Many organizations that have not been certified to OHSAS 18001 will have a program in place to analyze hazards and risks in the workplace and will have a process to ensure compliance with the legal regulations related to their operations. Those organizations can collect this information in support of the above process model before engaging in steps to conform to ISO 45001:2018 terminology. The goal should be to establish and maintain a safe workplace, while complying with regulations established to protect workers. Becoming certified to the ISO 45001:2018 standard provides verification of the organization's OH&S performance by a third-party certification body (CB), operating under guidelines and rules established by the ISO.

For organizations currently certified to OHSAS 18001:2007, this book will highlight and explain what is needed to satisfy the new requirements of ISO 45001:2018. The requirements new to ISO 45001:2018 are highlighted in boldface type. The full correspondence table between BS OHSAS 18001:2007 and ISO 45001:2018 is included in Appendix C.

The announcement by the American Society of Safety Engineers in Figure 3.3 heralded the introduction of the international standard for occupational health and safety: ISO 45001:2018. The number of fatalities worldwide from work-related incidents and illnesses is staggering. In the United States, there have been approximately 5000 workplace fatalities each year from 2014 to 2017. In 1970, when the Occupational Safety and Health Administration (OSHA) was created, 14,000 American workers had died on the job as a result of injury or ill health. Safety laws that reduced workplace fatalities by 65% in the United States during the last several decades is a notable achievement, but there are still too many workers dying on the job—in the United States and worldwide.

OSHA brought a level of discipline to the workplace in America in 1970. Many employers at the time believed, and still believe today, that OSHA is governmental overreach. Worker advocates and others disagree, pointing out that OSHA standards have been an important factor in the dramatic decline in worker injury and illness rates in many industries over the past decades. ISO 45001, although lacking

---

New Global Standard Considered a Milestone in Creating Safer Workplaces

PARK RIDGE, Illinois—Every day around the world, more than 7,600 lives are lost due to work-related incidents and diseases. That's nearly 2.8 million fatalities a year. To combat this global safety issue, a new safety standard has been approved after five years in the making—ISO 45001 Occupational Health and Safety Management Systems, spearheaded by the International Organization for Standardization (ISO) with support from the American Society of Safety Engineers (ASSE). The voluntary consensus standard provides a framework that can increase employee safety, reduce workplace risks and improve business outcomes worldwide.

The first-of-its-kind global consensus model for managing safety and health risks is expected to be published in March. ASSE played a key role in the seven-stage process that began in 2013, serving as the administrator of the U.S. technical advisory group (TAG) to the American National Standards Institute (ANSI). According to ISO, 93 percent of its members voted in favor of the new international standard, far above the requirement of a two-thirds majority.

"ISO 45001 is one of the most significant developments in workplace safety over the past 50 years, presenting an opportunity to move the needle on reducing occupational safety and health risks," said TAG Chair Vic Toy, CSP and CIH. "The goal was to create a widely accepted standard that can produce a highly effective safety and health management system for an increasingly interconnected world, regardless of an organization's size, location, supply chains or nature of work. It becomes a minimum standard of practice, and a good one at that."

Figure 3.3 Benefits of ISO 45001:2018.

Source: American Society of Safety Engineers, January 31, 2018, http://www.asse.org/new-global-standard-considered-a-milestone-in-creating-safer-workplaces/.

the clout of OSHA, can also provide some discipline to organizations seeking occupational health and safety audits and third-party certification.

A robust hazards and risk program and formalized worker safety training and awareness, along with increased worker participation, are all required by ISO 45001 and should be helpful in improving workplace safety. Ensuring contractors working at a company's property are educated about the company's safety requirements is also required by the ISO 45001 standard. For ISO 45001 to "move the needle in reducing occupational safety and health risks," certified organizations will also need a paradigm shift, in my opinion. Management will have to embrace and support a *continual improvement culture* in their occupational health and safety management system, creating an atmosphere where employees understand that working safely is priority number one. Continuing safety improvement is a requirement of ISO 45001.

I have been in plants where a proactive safety culture was evident. In a large chemical plant manufacturing highly reactive chemicals in the Houston area, I was required to view a one-hour safety video and be trained on the use of a self-contained breathing apparatus before I could start my audit and plant tour. Should the alarm sound while I was between buildings, I was advised how to use the windsock to determine which direction to take to escape the possible release of dangerous vapors to plan my escape. I was accompanied everywhere by an escort, right up to the door of the men's room. I was at the location for three days. Each morning at 7:00 a.m., I attended the environmental-safety review of the previous day. Workers would discuss potential safety issues and thank their peers as appropriate for assistance. The motivation for this approach was obvious: work safely, or your life is at risk. I felt the management and work force had established a "safety first" culture.

At another location, a large contract manufacturer producing electronic components in Guadalajara, Mexico, I audited the company's environmental and safety management systems as part of multisite certification. The hazards and risks were very low, but I was pleased to observe a proactive safety culture. When an accident occurred in the plant, the safety team would provide posters or similar visuals to highlight the causal factors and communicate the information to all 4000 employees to provide a heads-up and avoid a similar incident elsewhere. In some cases the information would be forwarded to the corporate safety director for circulation to other worldwide locations. The Mexican workers may have been motivated by having a job with a good company, but, after a while, I believe the positive safety atmosphere was self-sustaining. Of the dozen or more plants I audited for the same company, the Guadalajara plant had the best safety (and environmental) management system. Other locations also were in low-wage countries, but somehow the Guadalajara management and workers had found a culture of safety.

I believe ISO 45001:2018 implementation can be helpful in "moving the needle on reducing occupational safety and health risks" by adding the discipline of the ISO concept; but organizations will also need to embrace a culture of "safety first" for a major improvement to take place. I like to think of managing a safe workplace as a "three-legged stool" (Figure 3.4).

I have been in many plants where management and the employees have found this "safety first" culture. It is rewarding to see the "zero lost time accidents for 735 days" signs proudly posted and to see a clean, orderly plant with workers using their safety glasses and other protective gear. In other plants, I was often dismayed to observe sloppy housekeeping and a lack of safety enforcement. My auditor

Figure 3.4   Three-legged stool.

colleagues and I would often predict the results of the audit based on observations during the plant tour. If the organization cannot keep a clean and orderly plant, why would we expect the company to produce an excellent quality product and maintain a safe workplace?

Management needs to provide the *support* for an effective OH&S; implementation of an ISO 45001:2018 conforming management system can provide the *discipline* to sustain a safe workplace. But a company can have management support and be ISO 45001 certified—but will not be completely successful in maintaining a safe workplace unless management and workers find the "safety first" *culture*.

Chapter 10 of this handbook describes some programs an organization can use to continually improve their OH&S management system.

ISO 45001:2018 OCCUPATIONAL HEALTH AND SAFETY MANAGEMENT SYSTEMS: REQUIREMENTS WITH GUIDANCE FOR USE

Scope

This document specifies requirements for an occupational health and safety (OH&S) management system, and gives guidance for its use, to enable organizations to provide safe and healthy workplaces, by preventing work-related injury and ill health, as well as by proactively improving its OH&S performance.

This document is applicable to any organization that wishes to establish, implement and maintain an OH&S management system to improve occupational health and safety, eliminate hazards and minimize OH&S risks (including system deficiencies), take advantage of OH&S opportunities, and address OH&S management system nonconformities associated with its activities.

This document helps an organization to achieve the intended outcomes of its OH&S management system. Consistent with the organization's OH&S policy, the intended outcomes of an OH&S management system include:

- Continual improvement of OH&S performance

- Fulfillment of legal requirements and other requirements

- Achievement of OH&S objectives

This document is applicable to any organization regardless of its size, type and activities. It is applicable to the OH&S risks under the organization's control, taking into account factors such as the context in which the organization operates and the needs and expectations of its workers and other interested parties.

This document does not state specific criteria for OH&S performance, nor is it prescriptive about the design of an OH&S management system.

This document enables an organization, through its OH&S management system, to integrate other aspects of health and safety, such as worker wellness/well-being.

This document does not address issues such as product safety, property damage, or environmental impacts, beyond the risks to workers and other relevant interested parties.

This document can be used in whole or in part to systematically improve occupational health and safety management. However, claims of conformity to this document are not acceptable unless all its requirements are incorporated into an organization's OH&S management system and fulfilled without exclusion.

Normative References

There are no normative references in this document.

Terms and Definitions

For the purposes of this document, the following terms and definitions apply. ISO and IEC maintain terminological databases for use in standardization at the following addresses:

- ISO Online browsing platform: available at https://www.iso.org/obp

- IEC Electropedia: available at http://www.electropedia.org

Author Note

The definitions from ISO 45001:2018 are listed in Appendix A in alphabetical order.

4
Context of the Organization

#	ISO 45001:2018	#	OHSAS 18001:2007
4	Context of the organization	4	OH&S management system requirements (title only)
4.1	Understanding the organization and its context	4.1	General requirements
4.2	**Understanding the needs and expectations of workers and other interested parties**		NEW
4.3	Determining the scope of the OH&S management system	4.1	General requirements
4.4	OH&S management system	4.1	General requirements

4.1–4.2 Understanding the Organization and Its Context

The organization shall define:

- External and internal issues that are relevant to the organization's ability to provide a framework for managing the organization's OH&S risks to prevent work-related injury and ill health to workers;
- The needs and expectations of the organization's workers and other interested parties that can impact the organization's OH&S;
- Current or potential legal requirements and other requirements related to the organization's OH&S.

4.3 Determining the Scope of the OH&S Management System

In consideration of the context of the organization's OH&S, work-related activities, and boundaries of applicability, the organization shall document its scope.

4.4 OH&S Management System

The organization shall establish, maintain, and continually improve an OH&S management system, including the processes needed and their interactions, in accordance with the requirements of ISO 45001:2018.

4.1–4.2 UNDERSTANDING THE ORGANIZATION AND ITS CONTEXT (NEW CLAUSE)

The previous OHSAS 18001:2007 standard required organizations to define the *scope*—the activities, processes, and buildings and property within their occupational health and safety management system. The new clauses of ISO 45001:2018 ("Understanding the Organization and Its Context" and "Understanding the Needs and Expectations of Interested Parties") require the organization to analyze all issues that can have an impact on the organization's OH&S. These new clauses are consistent with the requirement that company quality management (ISO 9001:2015) and environmental management (ISO 14001:2015) now view their business from a more holistic, proactive vantage point. In this case *context* refers to the organization's business model, the external and internal issues that can impact the company.

There are many *external* issues that can have an impact on an organization's business: new regulations, the economy, new technology, competition, worker availability, and availability of qualified suppliers and contractors. *Internal issues* that can impact the organization include new materials and products, new processes, equipment, worker representatives, worker language, and worker capabilities. Interested parties can include regulatory agencies, industry sectors, customers, workers, neighbors, and the community.

The internal/external issues and interested parties that have an impact on an organization's OH&S management system are somewhat limited and are similar for companies of all sizes and complexities. To satisfy the requirement of clauses 4.2 and 4.3, an organization can establish a *context* checklist indicating what the potential issues are, which ones apply to its business model, and what actions may be appropriate. To illustrate the process, I have filled out the checklist from the vantage point of a chemical manufacturing company (Figure 4.1).

Each item that could have an impact on the company's OH&S management system should be addressed. A third-party auditor would expect the organization to provide follow-up actions as appropriate to the issues. When there are issues related to confidentiality, the organization should inform the auditor and redact the information. An experienced auditor respects the confidentiality and assesses whether the organization has a process in place to *understand the context and interested parties* relative to their OH&S.

4.3 DETERMINING THE SCOPE OF THE OH&S MANAGEMENT SYSTEM

Scope

The scope is what the organization does; the products or services the organization provides. For example, for the chemical manufacturer mentioned previously the scope is "Design and Manufacture of Specialty Chemicals."

The scope is defined in the organization's OH&S management system, but more information is needed to describe the boundaries of the organization's responsibilities and the context of its commitments.

Context Checklist:		Reviewed: Jan. 1, 2018
Possible external issues?	**Y/N**	**Actions/comments**
Worker protection regulations	y	Continue updating new safety data sheets
Technology	y	Purchase improved eyewash stations
Other	n	
Possible internal issues?		
New material	y	Establish chemical review approval process
New products	y	Establish chemical review approval process
New processes	n	
New equipment	y	New shrink-wrap machine; capital approval form covered safety sign-off
Worker representatives	n	No change FY 2017
Worker language	y	Continue English as second language class
Worker capabilities	n	
Other	n	
Interested parties		
Regulatory agencies	y	See safety committee annual OSHA review
Industry sectors	y	Sales reviewing possible membership ACC
Customers	n	No new customer safety directors
Workers	n	Expanding worker inputs JSA
Neighbors	y	Possible issue with loading-dock noise
Community	y	Safety engineer attended town meeting regarding chlorine deliveries
Other	n	

Figure 4.1   Sample context checklist.

Boundary

The scope defines the spatial and organizational boundaries to which the OH&S management system will apply, especially if the organization is a part of a larger organization at a given location. How many sites (building addresses) are under the scope? Who owns the property? If the organization does not own the site(s), but leases the properties from a landlord (leaseholder), then the responsibilities for the organization and landlord need to be defined. What are the boundaries? Are there manufacturing or service groups located on the organization's site that are not in the scope of the OH&S? The organization needs to define health and safety issues under its control and responsibility.

The boundaries and site ownership should not be considered a form of "exclusion" of responsibility for protection of any worker or individual, either on or near the organization's property. When an organization has employees from another organization working on the premises, their safety (and the impact on the organization's workers) has to be addressed. For example, when a company outsources the making of chemicals or ink to another company in a section of the organization's plant. There will be situations created by the other company's workers that could impact the health and safety of the workers of the parent organization.

In the case where the organization leases the property from another company, the organization has responsibility to ensure its processes or activities do not have an adverse workplace safety impact on the lease holder's personnel or property. The renting organization and the owner of the property need to coordinate communication on fire safety, evacuation drills, and other worker safety issues.

Some of the considerations that need to be addressed for an ISO 45001:2018–certified organization with multiemployer/employee workplaces include fire and other emergencies, management of potential chemical exposures, fork truck traffic safety, and personal protective equipment (PPE).

The responsibilities, restrictions, and agreements for multiemployee workplaces should be documented in the organization's OH&S MS Manual or similar document. In some cases, signed agreements may be required to ensure clear communications and implementation of requirements/policies/regulations related to all individuals employed at the site or complex.

Multiemployee sites present a high potential for accidents or injuries if responsibilities and communications are not clearly defined and controlled. A third-party auditor must dig deeply into the arrangements and audit the implementation actions, including the testing of the plans, when at a multisite location.

4.4 OH&S MANAGEMENT SYSTEM

Clause 4.4 is one of the mandatory clauses required by Annex SL:

> The organization shall establish, implement, maintain and continually improve an OH&S management system, including the processes needed and their interactions, in accordance with the requirements of this document.

This clause was established in 2000 when the quality standard ISO 9001 began to promote process management as key to maintaining an effective quality management system, requiring organizations to define the management system processes and their interactions. ISO 9001:2015 clause 4.4 contains the above first sentence but further defines the requirement:

> The organization shall determine the processes needed for the quality management system and their application throughout the organization, and shall:
>   a) Determine the inputs required and the outputs expected from these processes;
>   b) Determine the sequence and interaction of these processes.

I believe clause 4.4 is a force fit on ISO 45001 (and ISO 14001). The evidence the organization conforms to this clause will be demonstrated by conformance to all the other clauses of ISO 45001. However, in working with clients certifying to the environmental standard ISO 14001:2015, I discovered that the registrars (certification bodies) are requiring their third-party auditors to take the clause literally, expecting organizations to include a process flowchart of the environmental management system documentation.

How can an organization satisfy this requirement? They could include the process interaction chart from their quality management system. The quality processes of sales, design, and so on, do not directly interact with the OH&S

management system processes, so that chart would not help the organization improve their OH&S.

The organization could copy and paste plan-do-check-act from the introduction of the ISO 45001:2018 standard (Figure 4.2). I witnessed many organizations using a similar chart to satisfy the process interaction chart for their quality management systems. I would inform the auditee that the PDCA chart represents the processes and interaction of the major clauses of ISO 9001, which are the same whether the organization makes nuts and bolts or rocketships: no value.

Many organizations have been certified (by the British Standards Institute) to OHSAS 18001. They have established a strong OH&S management system. The safety of their workers won't be improved by inclusion of a process-interaction flowchart. Figure 4.3 shows a flowchart describing the interactions of ISO 45001 that I believe is more detailed than Figure 4.2.

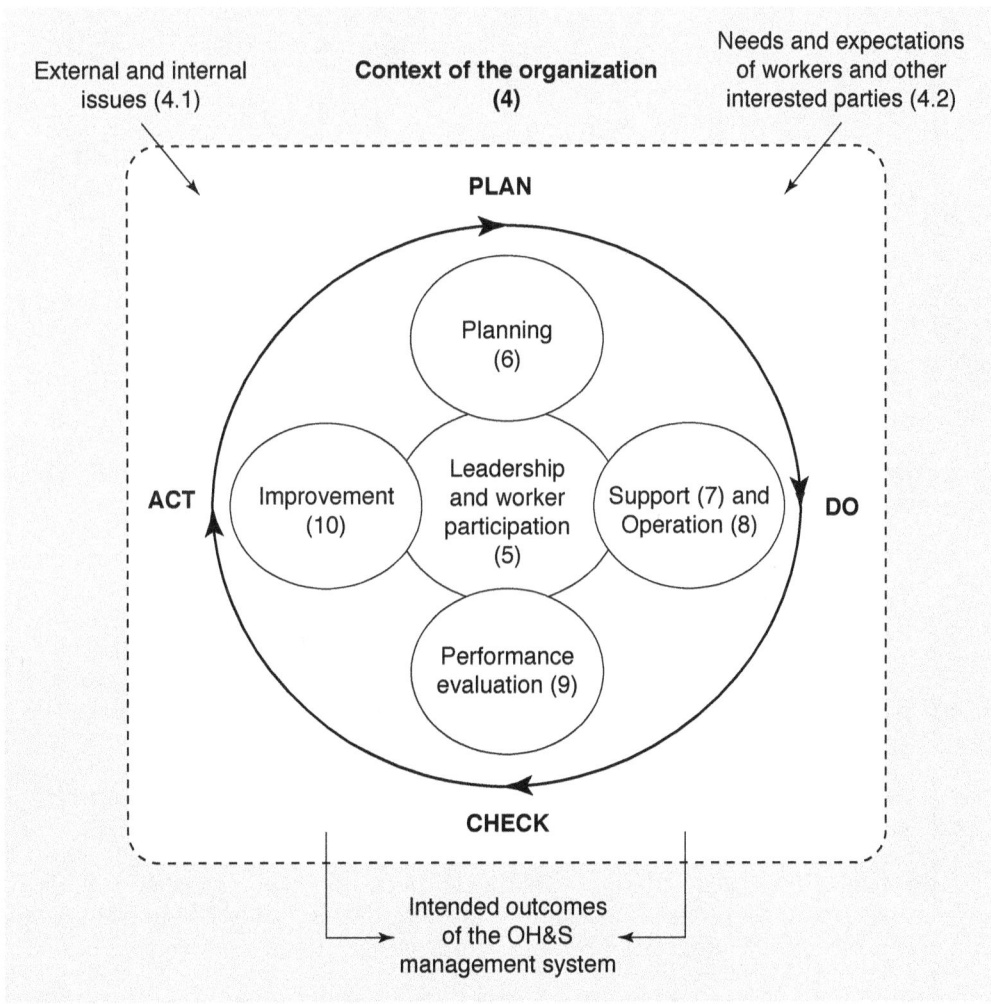

Figure 4.2 Relationship between PDCA and the framework of this international standard.
Source: ISO 45001:2018.

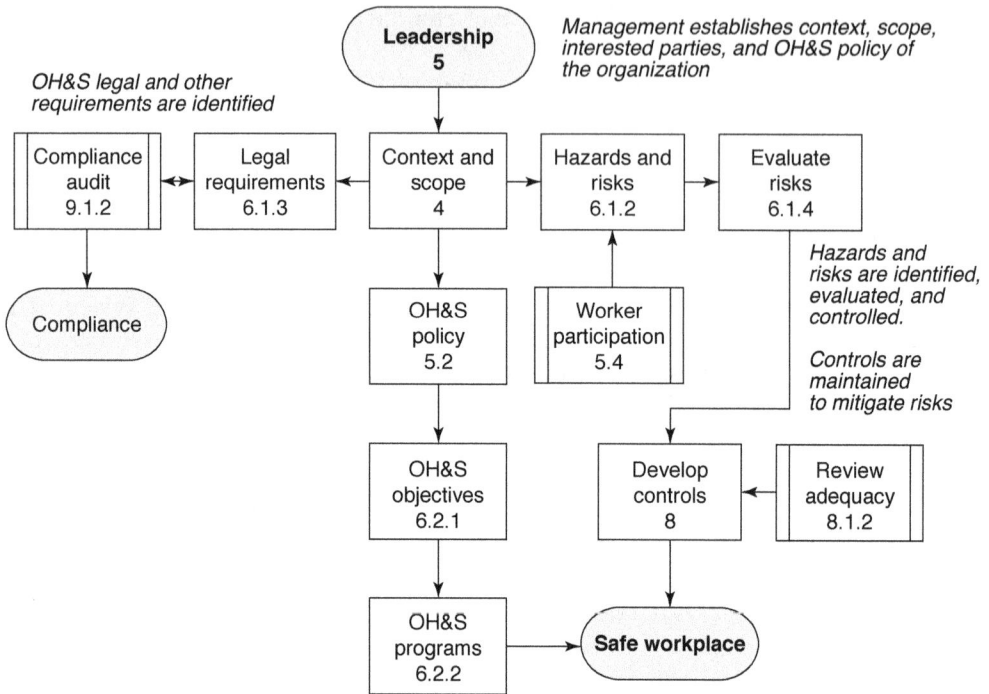

Figure 4.3   The occupational health and safety management system as a process, with standard sections noted.

This chart could be used by any company, so its value may be in making employees aware of the main clauses of an OH&S management system, and possibly satisfying poorly trained third-party auditors.

Internal Audit Questions

4.1–4.4 Understanding the Organization and Its Context

How has the organization defined the external and internal issues that can affect, either positively or negatively, the way the organization manages its OH&S responsibilities? What are these issues?

How has the organization identified the issues related to interested parties (customers, communities, neighbors) related to the organization's OH&S? What are they?

How has the organization defined and documented the scope of its OH&S management system? (Scope is defined as activities, products, and services of the organization to include all site addresses and buildings.)

Does the organization own the property? If not, how does the organization ensure that OH&S responsibilities are defined? Verify that boundaries for the site have been defined.

If organization leases areas of the site to other companies, define how the organization ensures the renter's activities do not have a negative impact on the organization's OH&S.

5

Leadership and Worker Participation

#	ISO 45001:2018	#	OHSAS 18001:2007
5	Leadership and worker participation	4	Implementation and operation
5.1	Leadership and commitment	4.4.1	Resources, roles, responsibility, accountability, and authority
5.2	**OH&S policy**	4.2	OH&S policy
5.3	Organizational roles, responsibilities and authorities	4.4.1	Resources, roles, responsibility, accountability, and authority
5.4	Consultation and participation of workers	4.4.3.2	Participation and consultation

5.1 Leadership and Commitment

Top management shall:

- Take overall responsibility and accountability for the prevention of work-related injury and ill health and provide safe and healthy workplaces and activities;
- Ensure that the OH&S policy and related OH&S objectives are established and are compatible with the strategic direction of the organization;
- Ensure the integration of the OH&S management system requirements into the organization's business processes;
- Ensure that the resources needed to establish, implement, maintain, and improve the OH&S management system are available;
- Communicate the importance of effective OH&S management and of conforming to the OH&S management system requirements;
- Ensure that the OH&S management system achieves its intended outcomes;
- Direct and support efforts of managers and workers to contribute to the effectiveness of the OH&S management system and to promote continual improvement of the OH&S;
- Protect workers from reprisals when reporting incidents, hazards, and risks;
- Ensure the organization establishes and implements processes for consultation and participation of workers and supports the establishment and functioning of health and safety committees.

5.1 LEADERSHIP AND COMMITMENT

This clause is the overarching statement of what is required of top management in supporting the organization's OH&S management system. The organization's management notes and performance records should indicate how effectively top management is leading the OH&S management system by providing the necessary resources, strategic direction, and communications to achieve the desired results.

While OHSAS 18001:2007 included commitment from management to support the OH&S management system, ISO 45001:2018 amplifies this commitment. ISO 45001:2018 emphasizes top management's responsibilities as more than delegating. Requirements are more specific to top management with regards to demonstrating leadership and commitment. The requirement *Take overall responsibility and accountability for the prevention of work-related injury and ill health and provide safe and healthy workplaces and activities* is quite clear. Top management of companies of any size is currently held accountable for the safety of its workers by OSHA (and similar agencies in most countries). ISO 45001:2018 requires third-party auditors to assess top management's performance.

Criticizing, or issuing nonconformances, against top management is a challenge for third-party auditors. My advice to auditors is to review the relevant safety metrics and programs of the organization being audited. If the goals for improvement and reduction of injuries are not being achieved, but management is providing resources, attending working sessions, and generally supporting improvement programs, then a nonconformance is usually not in order. If top management support is lacking, then a nonconformance may be issued, but the nonconformance should describe a *lack of effective (or missing) programs*, not a high number of accidents or injuries.

I have audited very few organizations where lack of top management support resulted in the issuance of a nonconformance. Lack of management support is the *ultimate major nonconformance* as it constitutes a breakdown of the management system. During an ISO 14001 environmental audit of a plant that was part of a multisite, international company, I found that the organization had not conducted internal audits for more than a year; they had not held management reviews; there were several lapses in their defined waste management controls. While there were underlying causes for these lapses in their management structure, a major nonconformance was issued. I returned to the plant a month later, accompanied by the company's corporate director of environmental affairs, to clear the nonconformances.

Many organizations, currently OHSAS 18001–certified, have integrated the OH&S management system into their business planning and strategy and woven the safety performance metrics into their business plan. The KPIs assigned to quality, environmental, and business parameters also include the safety metrics of accidents and safety incidents and "near-misses." "Best-in-class" organizations have established a business management system (BMS) incorporating their financial, quality, and environmental systems into a cohesive operational model with *safety* often appearing as the first agenda item.

Top management's role in supporting worker participation in the OH&S management system will be demonstrated by the effectiveness of the various reports related to analyzing hazards and risks and improvement opportunities. If there are gaps in worker involvement, nonconformance with clause 5.4 ("Consultation and Participation of Workers") may be issued relating to the organization's lack of implementation of clause 5.4. There may not be any value in referring to lack of top management support in worker participation unless there are other obvious examples also indicating absence of top management support.

Issuing a nonconformance against top management may be warranted as described in the example in the environmental audit cited previously.

Assessing whether the organization "protects workers from reprisals when reporting incidents, hazards, risks and opportunities" is outside the scope of a third-party ISO 45001:2018 audit, in my opinion, as the issue can have serious legal consequences.

Internal Audit Questions

5.1 Leadership and Commitment

How has top management supported the establishment of the OH&S policy and objectives?

How has top management integrated the OH&S policy and objectives into the strategic direction, business processes, and the context of the organization?

What is the evidence to indicate that top management provides resources to support the OH&S management system?

5.2 OH&S policy

Top management shall establish, document, and maintain an OH&S policy, specific to the nature of its OH&S risks and OH&S opportunities that:

- Includes a commitment to provide safe and healthy working conditions for the prevention of work-related injury and ill health;
- Is appropriate to the purpose, size, and context of the organization;
- Provides a framework for setting the OH&S objectives;
- Includes a commitment to fulfill legal requirements and other requirements;
- Includes a commitment to eliminate hazards and reduce OH&S risks;
- Includes a commitment to continual improvement of the OH&S management system;
- Includes a commitment to consultation with, and participation of, workers and workers' representatives, if applicable. The OH&S policy shall be communicated within the organization and available to interested parties as appropriate.

5.2 OH&S POLICY

The OH&S Policy can be a very concise statement of the organization's commitment to maintaining a safe workplace or, as some organizations choose, it can be a longer outline of their mission to ensure the safety of their employees. Often, the OH&S policy is combined with the environmental policy for organizations that

---

Occupational Health & Safety Policy

The Smith Coating Company is committed to protecting the health and safety of our employees and the individuals engaged in activities at our facilities. Smith Coating Company will:

- Comply with applicable occupational health and safety laws, regulations, and other requirements related to the maintenance of a safe workplace;
- Provide safe and healthy working conditions for the prevention of work-related injury and ill health;
- Commit to elimination of hazards and reduction of OH&S risks;
- Consult with workers on issues relating to OH&S and encourage their participation; and
- Commit to continual improvement of the OH&S management system.

The OH&S policy has been communicated within the organization and to persons doing work under Smith Coating Company's control as applicable. The policy will be made available to external interested parties upon request.

Company President   January 12, 2018

Figure 5.1   Example OH&S policy.

maintain an environmental health and safety (EH&S) program. This policy can be effective and simplify communications with employees. The EH&S policy is sometimes combined with the organization's quality policy. In my opinion, this can be confusing. An example of an OH&S policy for the Smith Coating Company is shown in Figure 5.1. I'll use the Smith Coating Company throughout this handbook to demonstrate the application of other clause requirements of ISO 45001:2018.

The organization will need to maintain a process to communicate the policy to employees, individuals working on its behalf, and interested parties. If the organization has a website, the policy can be posted.

Internal Audit Questions

5.2 OH&S Policy

Does the policy include

- A commitment to continual improvement?
- A commitment to provide safe and healthy working conditions for the prevention of work-related injury and ill health?
- A commitment to comply with applicable legal and other requirements?
- A commitment to eliminate hazards and reduce OH&S risks?
- A commitment to consultation with, and participation of, workers?

Is the policy documented, signed, and dated?

How is it communicated to employees, temporary help, and contractors?

How is it made available to the public?

5.3 Organizational Roles, Responsibilities and Authorities

Top management shall ensure that the responsibilities and authorities for relevant roles within the OH&S management system are assigned, documented, and communicated at all levels within the organization.

Workers at each level of the organization shall assume responsibility for those aspects of OH&S management system over which they have control.

Top management shall assign the responsibility and authority for:

- Ensuring that the OH&S management system conforms to the requirements of ISO 45001:2018;
- Reporting the performance of the OH&S management system to top management.

5.3 ORGANIZATIONAL ROLES, RESPONSIBILITIES, AND AUTHORITIES

The organization's documentation should define individual responsibility and authority for maintaining the OH&S management system. Examples may include:

- Responsibility for:
  — Reporting the performance of the OH&S management system
  — Inspecting safety equipment
  — Procuring personal protective equipment
  — Conducting safety inspections

- Authority for:
  — Communicating with regulatory bodies and the public
  — Releasing OSHA injury reports
  — Approving reports to regulatory bodies

It is important to understand the difference between *authority* and *responsibility*. In the business context, responsibility is the obligation of a subordinate to perform the duty as required by his or her supervisor. The person accepting responsibility is accountable for the performance of the assigned duties. Authority is the power assigned to an executive or a manager in order to achieve certain organizational objectives. In the case of occupational health and safety management, the organization needs to be clear on who has the authority to ensure that information released to the state or federal government is accurate.

Many organizations bestow the responsibility to manage the OH&S on the safety manager. The safety manager and the plant manager, or highest authority at the site, then share the authority for releasing reports or documents to the state or federal agencies.

Internal Auditor Questions

5.3 Organizational Roles, Responsibilities and Authorities

Who (job title) has the responsibility and authority for ensuring that the OH&S management system conforms to the requirements of ISO 45001:2018?

Who (job title) has the authority for:

- Communicating with regulatory bodies and the public
- Releasing OSHA injury reports
- Approving reports to regulatory bodies

How are responsibilities and authorities documented within the OH&S MS?

5.4 Consultation and Participation of Workers

The organization shall establish, document, and maintain a process for consultation with, and participation of, workers at all applicable levels and functions and with workers' representatives, if applicable, in the development, planning, implementation, performance evaluation, and actions for improvement of the OH&S management system. The organization shall:

- Provide mechanisms, time, training, and resources necessary for worker consultation and participation;
- Provide timely access to clear, understandable, and relevant information about the OH&S management system;
- Define and remove obstacles or barriers to participation and minimize those that cannot be removed;
- Emphasize consultation with nonmanagerial workers on defining the needs and expectations of interested parties in establishing the OH&S policy and providing inputs to the OH&S as appropriate;
- Emphasize the participation of nonmanagerial workers in defining the mechanisms for their consultation and participation in identifying and eliminating hazards and assessing risks and opportunities;
- Provide workers the opportunity to assist OH&S in defining:
  - Competence requirements, training needs, and evaluation of training;
  - What needs to be communicated and the communication process;
  - Control measures and their effective implementation and use;
  - The process for investigating incidents and nonconformities and for defining/implementing corrective actions.

5.4 CONSULTATION AND PARTICIPATION OF WORKERS

The companies I audited for the OHSAS 18001 standard had a mixed range of worker involvement and participation. At the low end, the organization would assign an individual to represent the workforce in discussions of safety issues with management. The meeting notes would document discussions and agreements related to work hazards and reporting causes of injuries. On the high end of participation, the work group and supervision would meet weekly to discuss safety and review accidents, improvement projects, and near-misses, maintaining detailed notes. Safety-teams reenactments of accidents (safely) that occurred either in the group or elsewhere in the company helped to identify possible causes so preventive actions could be identified.

To assist the organizations preparing for ISO 45001:2018 certification, I suggest gathering evidence to indicate conformance with clause 5.4 ("Consultation and Participation of Workers") requirements as shown in Table 5.1.

When assessing an organization's conformance with clause 5.4 ("Consultation and Participation of Workers"), I suggest the auditor consider using a *grade* of A, B, or C.

If there is evidence of worker participation in the majority of the requirements, workers get an "A" grade; they are conforming. An organization conforming to 75% of requirements receives a "B" grade and might benefit from an opportunity to find ways to expand their workers' participation. An organization with scant evidence of worker participation earns a "C" grade, and the auditor will, most likely, issue a nonconformance. Of particular concern would be the situation where workers had little input into the identification of hazards in their work areas.

Many of my auditor colleagues will not accept this grading approach; however, assessing an organization's commitment to worker participation using more than a dozen requirements is unrealistic, in my opinion, particularly when an auditor is expected to evaluate if management is effective in *emphasizing* consultation regarding the needs and expectations of interested parties; auditors can have difficulty assessing requirements that include subjective terms.

Table 5.1 Worker participation examples of conformance.

Requirement	Examples
Provide timely access to clear, understandable, and relevant information about the OH&S management system.	• OH&S presentations during department or companywide meetings; • OH&S postings on bulletin boards
Define and remove obstacles or barriers to participation, and minimize those that cannot be removed.	• Provide time away from work stations for OH&S activities; • Provide multilingual reports
Emphasize the consultation of nonmanagerial workers on defining the needs and expectations of interested parties, establishing the OH&S policy, and providing inputs to the OH&S as appropriate.	"Emphasize" is difficult to assess, so this requirement may be satisfied by management statement of intent.
Provide workers the opportunity to assist OH&S in defining: • Competence requirements, training needs, and evaluation of training • What needs to be communicated and the communication process • Control measures and their effective implementation and use • Processes for investigation of incidents and nonconformities and defining/implementing corrective actions	**Evidence** • Workers sign off on job descriptions • Worker review of job safety during performance reviews • Worker input related to the OH&S during department or companywide meetings • Worker input for hazard analysis and job safety analysis • Worker participation in incident investigations

Internal Auditor Questions

5.4 Consultation and Participation of Workers

How does management provide access to relevant information about the OH&S?

How does management remove obstacles or barriers to participation?

How does management support consulting with workers about defining the needs and expectations of interested parties?

What is the evidence that workers have input to establishing:

- Training needs and evaluation of training
- The communication process
- Operational control measures
- Process for investigation of incidents

6
Planning

#	ISO 45001:2018	#	OHSAS 18001:2007
6	Planning	4.3	Planning
6.1	**Actions to address risks and opportunities**		NEW
6.1.1	**General**		
6.1.2	Hazard identification and assessment of risks and opportunities	4.3.1	Hazard identification, risk assessment, and determine controls
6.1.3	Determination of legal requirements and other requirements	4.3.2	Legal and other requirements
6.1.4	Planning action		
6.2	Objectives and planning to achieve them		
6.2.1	OH&S objectives	4.3.3	Objectives and programme(s)
6.2.2	**Planning to achieve OH&S objectives**		NEW

6.1 Actions to Address Risks and Opportunities

Within the context and scope of its OH&S management system, the organization shall define and document the risks and opportunities that need to be addressed to prevent work-related injury and ill health to workers and continually to improve the safe operations of the organization's workplace.

In defining the risks and opportunities, consideration shall be given to workplace hazards and the legal requirements applicable to the organization's OH&S Management system.

When changes in processes, machinery, equipment, and personnel occur, the organization shall assess the hazards and risks created by the change before implementing the change.

Hazard Identification

The organization shall establish, document, and maintain a process for hazard identification that is ongoing and proactive. The process shall take into account:

- Social and human factors;
- Routine and nonroutine activities;
- Infrastructure, equipment, materials, substances, and the physical conditions of the workplace;
- Product- and service-related activities:
  - Design, research, and development;
  - Production, assembly, and testing;
  - Construction and maintenance;
  - Storage and delivery;
  - Disposal of product and waste materials.
- Relevant historical incidents, internal or external to the organization, including emergencies
- Individuals with access to the workplace, and their activities, including contractors, visitors, and other individuals present in the vicinity of the workplace that can be affected by the activities of the organization.

The organization shall include consideration of hazards generated by process changes, the design of the workplace, installation of machinery/equipment, and related operating procedures.

Assessment of OH&S Risks and Other Risks to the OH&S Management System

The organization shall establish, document, and maintain a process to assess OH&S risks from the identified hazards, while taking into account the effectiveness of existing controls.

The organization's methodology and criteria for the assessment of OH&S risks shall be defined and documented with respect to the scope, nature, and timing, ensuring the methodology is proactive rather than reactive and is applied in a systematic way.

Assessment of OH&S Opportunities and Other Opportunities to the OH&S Management System

The organization shall establish, document, and maintain a process to assess/evaluate OH&S opportunities to enhance OH&S performance relating to:

- Elimination of hazards and reduced OH&S risks when considering changes to the organization, its policies, processes, and activities;
- How the organization organizes the work environment to match worker capabilities.

6.1 ACTIONS TO ADDRESS RISKS AND OPPORTUNITIES

Responding to the requirements in clause 6.1 ("Actions to Address Risks and Opportunities)" will be instrumental in determining how well an organization achieves its goal of preventing work-related injuries and ill health to workers. Comprehensive identification of workplace hazards and associated risks is the cornerstone on which a successful OH&S management system is built.

6.1.2 Hazard Identification and Assessment of Risks and Opportunities

The hazards identification process step involves identifying all activities performed by individuals working under the control of the organization and the safety (and health) threats the activities or tasks present. All the various processes/functions of the organization as defined in the scope of the organization need to be part of the hazards review and must address the tasks relating to:

- Operational/manufacturing
- Contractors working at the site
- The materials and chemicals used in products
- State and/or federal regulations
- Changes in any of the above

The risk planning process can be illustrated as a flow chart with inputs and outputs as shown in Figure 6.1.

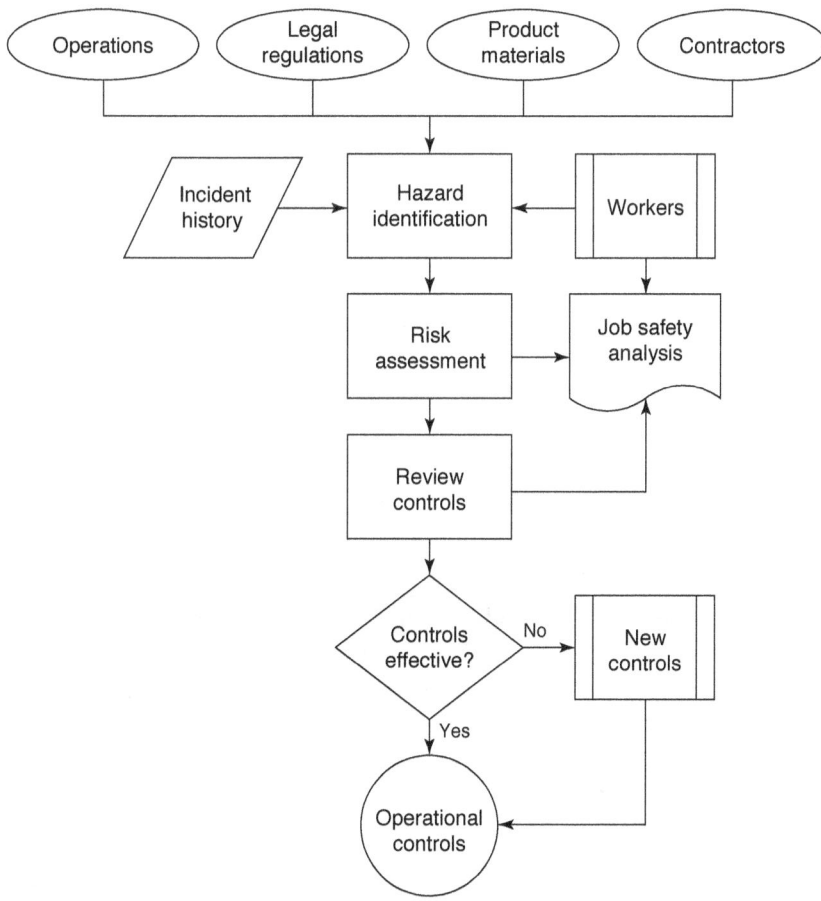

Figure 6.1   The risk-planning process.

Worker participation in defining the hazards relating to their tasks is required as previously described under clause 5.4 ("Consultation and Participation of Workers"). A review of the accidents and safety incidents that have occurred in the work areas can be helpful in the analytical process..

After the hazards have been identified, the risk level of the various tasks can be analyzed and prioritized, allowing evaluation of the effectiveness of the current controls. A technique commonly used to analyze hazards, risks, and controls is the job safety analysis (JSA).

To illustrate how a JSA can be applied to an organization, the hazards-risk review for a manufacturing company, the Smith Coating Company, is outlined in Figure 6.2.

The processes in the company that may include tasks that present injury risks for the workers are shown in Table 6.1. There will be similar risks relating to tasks in packaging, receiving, and shipping areas, and in laboratories and with maintenance.

Once the potential injury lists have been developed using input from the operators or workers in each process, the potential hazards to the individual can be identified for each task. For example, in lifting chemicals and unloading packages,

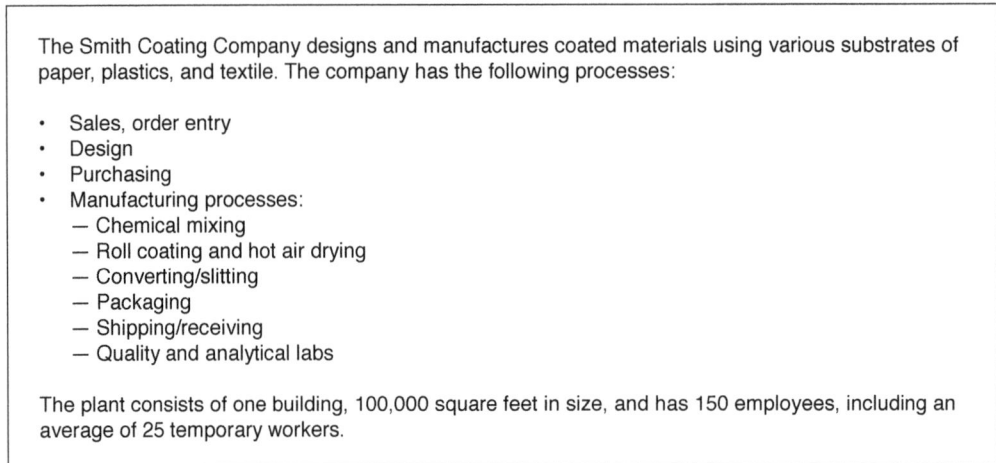

The Smith Coating Company designs and manufactures coated materials using various substrates of paper, plastics, and textile. The company has the following processes:

- Sales, order entry
- Design
- Purchasing
- Manufacturing processes:
  — Chemical mixing
  — Roll coating and hot air drying
  — Converting/slitting
  — Packaging
  — Shipping/receiving
  — Quality and analytical labs

The plant consists of one building, 100,000 square feet in size, and has 150 employees, including an average of 25 temporary workers.

Figure 6.2 Smith Coating Company processes.

Table 6.1 Smith Coating Company examples of tasks.

Chemical mixing tasks	Roll coating tasks	Converting/slitting rolls tasks
• Lifting chemical packages	• Using power equipment	• Using power equipment
• Dispensing materials	• Dispensing materials	• Changing blades
• Cleaning tanks	• Cleaning equipment	• Lifting rolls
• Working on mezzanine	• Threading webs into machine	• Adjusting machine
	• Lifting materials	• Threading machine
	• Adjusting machine	

there is the potential for injury to a worker's back or body. Additionally, the worker could be exposed to chemical burns or inhalation of toxic materials. A worker threading a web through the coating machine has the potential to have a body part entangled in the machine.

After the potential injury list is generated for all the various tasks and potential hazards, the next step is to define the existing controls and develop a risk level or potential for injury. This criterion can help determine the need for additional controls and an action plan to mitigate the risks. (Note: clause 8 will describe how the "hierarchy of controls" can be employed as part of this assessment.)

A technique used by many organizations is the JSA. In simple terms, a JSA identifies potential hazards and recommends the safest way to do the job. A properly designed and implemented JSA can be very effective in reducing workplace injuries and worker ill health. It is most effective when the level of worker participation in defining hazards and controls is high.

A comprehensive JSA will satisfy ISO 45001 clause 6.1.2 ("Hazard Identification and Assessment of Risks and Opportunities") requirements. An example of the JSA used by the Smith Coating Company is detailed in Figure 6.3.

There are many options for establishing a ranking system when evaluating the risks relating to the potential injuries a worker can be exposed to when performing various tasks. At the low end, an organization with few tasks exposing workers to injury might classify the risks as high, medium, or low. Using injury history and inputs from workers, the organization could prioritize actions that would promote and maintain a safe workplace. At the high end, an organization with extreme hazards in the workplace (e.g., mineral mining, toxic chemical manufacturing) may adopt a sophisticated failure mode effect analysis (FMEA) process as a quality tool, calculating a risk priority number (RPN).

There are programs (available on the internet) that have updated the conventional FMEA/RPN approach for prioritizing environmental, health and safety risks. One such example is the "total efficient risk priority number" (TERPN), which assists an organization in classifying risks to identify corrective actions that result in the highest risk reduction at the lowest cost.

JSA Worksheet				
Job: Chemical Mixing		**Prepared by: Mike**		**Date: Jan. 12, 2017**
Task	**Potential Hazard**	**Existing Controls**	**RPN**	**New controls?**
Lifting chemical packages	Back or body injury	Training hoist	60	
Dispensing materials	Chemical burn	PPE: Gloves, safety glasses	48	
	Material inhalation	PPE: Dust masks	24	
	Hand cut	PPE: Safety knives, gloves	12	
	Eye injury	PPE: Safety glasses	16	
Working on mezzanine	Fall	Guardrails	12	
	Injury to coworker	Safety helmet	16	

Figure 6.3 Smith Coating Company JSA worksheet.

I have used an RPN process that can be applied to a wide variety of industries in assessing the worker injury risks that is similar to the way in which organizations determine the ranking of their environmental aspects to determine which ones are *significant* and which help drive the organization's environmental activities. For example, an organization may have several activities (aspects) that impact the environment, such as management of waste, discharge of volatile compounds, or discharge of wastewater. The process is based on the equation,

$$RPN = severity \times likelihood \times control$$

Applied to an OH&S management system, the criteria for the Smith Coating Company and the assessment of the risk priority numbers for each task is shown in Table 6.2.

Returning to the example for JSA for Smith Coating and their chemical mixing tasks would result in the assessment of the risk priority numbers for each task shown in Table 6.3.

The Smith Coating Company would then establish actions to mitigate risks by adding new controls using the risk priority numbers as a driver along with other

Table 6.2   Severity/likelihood/control ranking

Severity	Criteria	Points	Likelihood	Frequency	Points	Control	Points
Very high	Life or limb	5	Very high	Daily	5	Strong	1
High	Hospital visit	4	High	Weekly	4	High	2
Medium	Lost time injury	3	Medium	Occasional	3	Medium	3
Low	OSHA recordable	2	Low	Seldom	2	Low	4
None	First aid	1	Remote	Infrequent	1	None	5

Table 6.3   Smith Coating Company RPN calculation.

Task	Severity	Likelihood	Control	RPN
Lifting chemical packages	4	5	3	60
Dispensing materials				
• Chemical burn	4	3	4	48
• Material inhalation	4	2	3	24
• Hand cut	3	2	2	12
• Eye injury	4	2	2	16
Working on mezzanine				
• Fall	5	2	4	40
• Injury to coworker	4	2	4	32

inputs such as history of accidents or near-misses in the area. Chapter 8, in the section discussing clause 8.1 ("Operational Planning and Control"), will provide guidance on reviewing the JSA and on establishing controls.

While the above job safety analysis outlines a baseline plan that can be helpful in reducing accidents, the process needs to be *dynamic* in nature to be successful. When identifying tasks with hazards, input from workers is necessary; however, it is useful to have an observer periodically witness the task the worker is performing to validate the potential hazards.

There are techniques that can be used to train observers to check both the physical condition (rushed, frustrated, fatigued, complacent) of the worker when doing a task as well as to note if some workers are making critical errors while performing a task. Chapter 10 will provide some options and links to providers of techniques for improving the analysis and reduction of workplace hazards.

While the job safety analysis can be used by an organization to conform to clause 6.1.2.1 ("Identification of Hazards"), clause 6.1.2.3 ("Assessment of OH&S Opportunities and Other Opportunities to the OH&S Management System") **also requires the organization to consider the risks of not reducing the hazards or in not** *achieving the opportunities to enhance OH&S performance.*

In my opinion, this requirement in ISO 45001:2018 is a form of "double jeopardy" or overreach. It is an artifact of Annex SL which requires all ISO management systems to address clause 6.1 ("Actions to Address Risks and Opportunities"). When the standards for the quality management system, ISO 9001:2015, and the environmental management system ISO 14001:2015 were issued, clause 6.1 generated a new concept in management systems, "risk management," to replace the much maligned requirement for *preventive actions.* When assisting clients in certifying to ISO 9001:2015 and ISO 14001:2015, I found these new risk analysis/management inclusion standards to be quite helpful in identifying the need for new controls. Their application to OH&S is shown in Table 6.4.

In the case of ISO 45001:2018, a comprehensive risk analysis, such as the job safety analysis applied by the Smith Coating Company, should satisfy the requirements of clause 6.1.2.3 as it relates to assessing obstacles to eliminating hazards and enhancing opportunities to improve the performance of the OH&S management system. A properly implemented JSA includes the assessment of the effectiveness of operational controls with the need to seek opportunities to improve controls if they are deemed important.

Table 6.4 OH&S risk assessment.

Task	Potential failure	Worker risk	Present controls	New controls?
Operating solvent paint booth	Lost ground connection, fire/explosion	Bodily injury	Preventive maintenance of static connections	Install in-duct gas monitor
Driving fork truck	Strike employee	Bodily injury	Training	Isolate employee traffic area

Internal Auditor Questions

6.1 Actions to Address Risks and Opportunities

What is the process the organization uses to define and address the hazards and risks in the workplace?

How are the workers involved in identifying the hazards in tasks they perform?

Were all manufacturing or servicing processes included in identifying hazards and risks?

How were the current controls evaluated as to how effective they were in reducing risk of injury due to the hazards?

What are the actions plans to improve controls to reduce the risks?

How does the organization assess the hazards and risks when there are changes in the organization's processes or equipment?

6.1.3 Determination of Legal Requirements and Other Requirements

The organization shall establish, document, and maintain a process that defines legal and other requirements applicable to its OH&S management system. The process shall include the method used to ensure that the legal and other requirements represent the current version of these requirements.

The organization shall review its OH&S legal and other requirements when changes or improvements are planned in the organization's processes or scope of activities.

The organization shall define how its legal and other requirements are communicated to workers and interested parties.

6.1.3 Determination of Legal Requirements and Other Requirements

The US Occupational Safety and Health Administration (OSHA) is an agency of the US Department of Labor. OSHA's mission is to prevent work-related injuries, illnesses, and occupational fatalities by issuing and enforcing standards for workplace safety and health, to create a better workplace for all workers, and to ensure the safety of everyone by making and enforcing certain standards that are needed to protect workers. The agency has the authority to create specific regulations for certain industries. Workplace safety is covered under 29 CFR (Code of Federal Regulations) Part 1910 (https://www.osha.gov/pls/oshaweb/owasrch.search_form?p_doc_type=STANDARDS&p_toc_level=1&p_keyvalue=1910). OSHA's website is user-friendly.

Clicking on the REGULATIONS tab for standard 1910 will provide links to the regulations relating to workplace safety. Most industrial sites will have 29 CFR Part 1910 regulations relating to general fire safety, exit signs, and doors, as well as to injury reporting. Depending on the processes at the site, other regulations may create requirements. To illustrate how an organization can conform to clause 6.1.3 ("Determination of Legal Requirements and Other Requirements"), the Smith Coating Company compiled the following list of activities or tasks that may be covered by OSHA regulations:

- Moving machinery

- Electrical devices

- Working at heights

- Handling chemicals

- Powered lift equipment

- Noise

The Smith Coating Company's legal list—a compilation of the regulations applicable to the organization's OH&S—is shown in Table 6.5.

Some states may have regulations that are stricter than OHSA's. Organizations should be cognizant of the workplace regulations for their state. As an example, the state of California has its own hazard communication standard or worker "right-to-know" law. The state's hazard communication standard differs from the federal standard OSHA 29 CFR 1910.1200. Organizations should list and follow the strictest regulation.

The legal list should be updated when processes and equipment are modified. A process to ensure the legal list is kept up to date is required. The OSHA link provided above will allow organizations to receive e-mail updates from OSHA.

"Other" Requirements Relating to the OH&S

There are nonregulatory groups and associations that have safety requirements that an organization may be subject to:

- Customers and customer advocacy groups

- Headquarters

- Local fire departments

- Insurance companies

- Industry sectors/associations

Examples for Smith Coating Company are shown in Table 6.6.

If the organization stores flammable materials, the local fire department may restrict the amount of chemicals on the site to limit the potential for fire/explosion that could endanger employees and the neighborhood. The fire department could also conduct inspections at the site. Likewise, the organization's insurance carrier could impose requirements and provide inspections at the site to ensure the organization is maintaining systems to protect the property from major physical losses and to eliminate sources of injury risks to employees.

Some customers or customer advocacy associations may require their suppliers to maintain safe operating standards. An example is bluesign technologies ag, located in Switzerland. This company is specifically geared toward the textile industry; but they do not function as an industry trade association. bluesign® is

Table 6.5   Smith Coating Company legal list.

Area	Regulatory source	Purpose	Requirement*
Injury recording	OSHA 29 CFR 1910.1904.7 Form 300	Require employers to record and report work-related fatalities, injuries, and illnesses	Record injury or illness; post-summary page at site
Servicing machines Lockout/tagout (LOTO)	OSHA 29 CFR 1910.147	Protect employees from harm caused by unexpected energization	Requires employers to establish a program and utilize procedures for affixing appropriate lockout devices
Machine guarding	OSHA 29 CFR 1910.212	Protect the operator and other employees in the machine area from hazards	Affix guards to the machine where possible and secure
Working at heights	OSHA 29 CFR 1910.28-29	Provide protection for each employee exposed to falling and falling object hazards	Provide and install all fall protection systems and falling object protection
Personal protective equipment (PPE)	OSHA 29 CFR 1910.132	Assess the workplace to determine if hazards are present which necessitate the use of personal protective equipment	Provide protective equipment for eyes, face, head, and extremities
Noise protection	OSHA 29 CFR 1910.95	Protect against the effects of noise exposure when the sound levels exceed certain levels	Provide personal protective equipment and require its use to reduce sound levels within the levels of the table
Tank entry	OSHA 29 CFR 1910.146	Protect employees in general industry from the hazards of entry into permit-required confined spaces	Evaluate the workplace to determine if any spaces are permit-required confined spaces
Chemical exposure	OSHA 29 CFR 1910.1200	Protect employees to injury due to exposure to chemicals	Develop, implement, and maintain at each workplace a written hazard communication program

*This is a partial list for demonstration purposes only. To see the complete regulation, access the OSHA website above for the particular 1910 part number.

better described as a certification body/certified company advocate promoting the bluesign® brand.

The bluesign® system unites the entire textile supply chain to reduce its negative impact on people and the environment. The organization requires member companies to observe certain environmental health and safety (EHS) criteria when producing materials in the textile supply chain. While membership is voluntary, organizations selling to textile customers (particularly in Europe) are required to become certified to bluesign®, including having a third-party audit.

Table 6.6 Smith Coating Company nonregulatory requirements.

Item	Source	Purpose	Requirement
Fire safety	Local fire department	Maintain safe workplace and community	Limit storage of flammable materials
Facilities	Insurance company	Protect employees and facilities	Safety inspections
Textile customers	bluesign®	Guarantee the application of sustainable ingredients in a clean process and safely manufactured product	Conformance to bluesign® criteria (www.bluesign.com)

I witnessed application of bluesign® criteria at a company manufacturing coated textiles. The bluesign® audit included many requirements consistent with ISO 14001:2015 and ISO 45001:2018. Organizations subject to EHS requirements imposed by customers will find ISO 45001:2018 certification very helpful. Other product sectors may follow the bluesign® model in the future.

Internal Auditor Questions

6.1.3 Determination of Legal Requirements and Other Requirements

How does the organization define the health and safety regulations that relate to the organization's activities or facilities?

Has the organization identified the federal and/or state regulations relating to its activities such as:

- Injury recording
- Servicing machines
- Lockout/tagout
- Machine guarding
- Working at heights
- PPE
- Noise protection
- Tank entry
- Chemical exposure
- Fire safety

What process does the organization use to ensure regulations meet the current requirements?

What other nonregulatory safety requirements is the organization subject to?

- Customer and customer advocacy groups
- Headquarters
- Local fire department
- Insurance companies
- Industry sectors/associations
- Other

6.1.4 Planning Action (New Clause)

The organization shall plan actions and controls to address the defined OH&S risks, opportunities, and legal requirements, and other requirements to establish appropriate controls and prepare for and respond to emergency situations in the OH&S management system.
   The organization shall define how it:

- Integrates the OH&S actions and controls into its other business processes;
- Evaluates the effectiveness of these actions;
- Takes into account the hierarchy of controls when planning to take action;
- Considers best practices, technological options, and financial, operational, and business requirements when planning actions and controls in its OH&S.

6.1.4 Planning Action

Clause 6.1.4 provides an overarching planning requirement about how the organization addresses the defined OH&S risks, legal requirements, operational controls, and emergency situations. The planning process can be outlined graphically as a "roadmap" (Figure 6.4).

   The response to the requirements for clause 6.1 ("Actions to Address Risks and Opportunities") indicated that an organization can use a job safety analysis process and documentation to satisfy this requirement. Similarly, the process used to determine and manage the OH&S legal and other requirements was outlined in section 6.1.3 ("Determination of Legal Requirements and Other Requirements"). Chapter 8, Operational Control, will describe how an organization can respond to requirements for operational controls and emergency planning and preparedness by using best practices, technological options, and financial, operational, and business requirements.

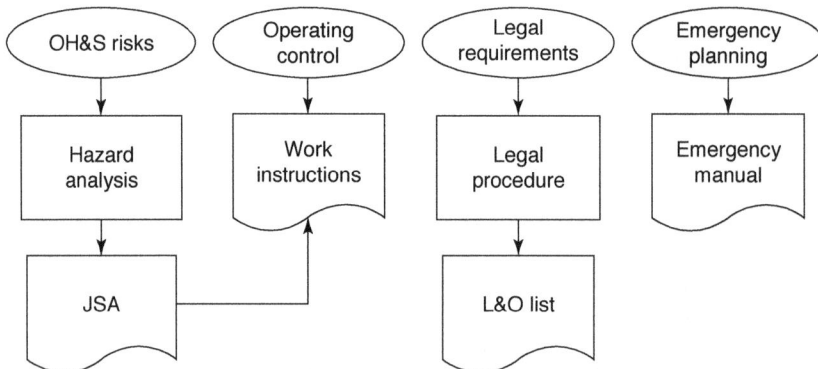

Figure 6.4   OH&S planning inputs and outputs.

Internal Auditor Questions

6.1.4 Planning Action

How does the organization integrate the OH&S actions and controls into its other business processes?

How does the organization take into account the "hierarchy of controls" when planning to take an action?

How does the organization consider best practices, technological options, and financial, operational, and business requirements when planning actions and controls for its OH&S?

6.2.1 OH&S Objectives

The organization shall establish and document OH&S objectives at relevant functions and levels in order to maintain and continually improve the OH&S management system and OH&S performance.

The OH&S objectives shall:

- Be consistent with the OH&S policy;
- Be measurable, if practicable, or be capable of performance evaluation;
- Take into account:
  ○ Applicable requirements;
  ○ The results of the assessment of risks and opportunities;
  ○ The results of consultation with workers and workers' representatives, if applicable.
- Be monitored;
- Be communicated to workers and interested parties, as applicable;
- Be updated as appropriate.

6.2.2 Planning to Achieve OH&S Objectives (New Clause)

When planning how to achieve its OH&S objectives, the organization shall define and document:

- What methods/techniques will be used to accomplish the objectives;
- What resources will be required;
- Who will be responsible;
- When it will be completed;
- How the results will be evaluated, including indicators for monitoring;
- How the actions to achieve OH&S objectives will be integrated into the organization's business processes.

6.2 OH&S OBJECTIVES AND PLANNING TO ACHIEVE THEM

The organization needs to establish measurable objectives and a process to monitor, communicate, and update the objectives. ISO 45001:2018 clause 6.1.4 ("Planning Action") requires the organization to take into account the legal requirements, OH&S risks, its technological options, and its financial, operational, and business requirements, and the views of relevant interested parties when establishing OH&S objectives. Additionally, the previous year's injury and accident history sets a baseline for improvement and is another valuable input. Graphically, the objective-setting process is shown in Figure 6.5.

To illustrate how the objective-setting process can work, the Smith Coating Company collected OH&S metrics from the previous year and reviewed proposed process changes for the coming year. Each department was tasked with meeting with workers to review their previous year's safety performance and to suggest ways to improve their department's safety performance. After consolidating the inputs, Smith Coating Company selected three OH&S objectives for 2018:

- Reduce the plant-wide OSHA recordable incident rate by 25%

- Purchase and install two new eyewash/shower units for the chemical mix department

- Update the roll-change hoist in the slitting department

Smith Coating Company had an uptick in OSHA incidents in 2017, so there was wide agreement in the plant to seek new techniques in reducing hand cuts, back injuries, and slips in the parking lot. The chemical mix area eyewashes were old; new units are easier to operate and test. There were two minor back injuries incurred by workers in the slitting operation.

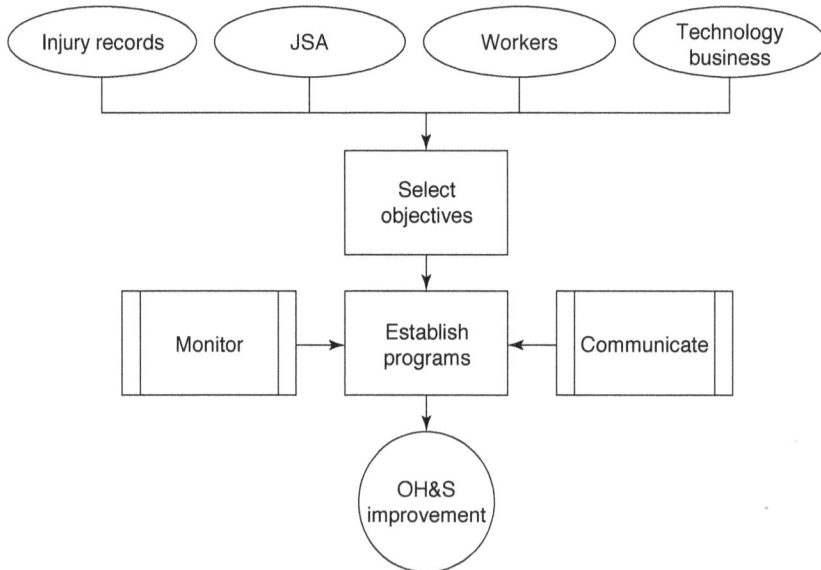

Figure 6.5   OH&S objective/program-selection process.

Internal Auditor Questions

6.2.1 OH&S Objectives

How were the OH&S objectives determined?

What are the current OH&S objectives?

Provide an example of an OH&S measurable objective with a quantifiable target (goal).

When establishing and reviewing objectives, how does the organization take into account:

- The legal requirements and other requirements
- The OH&S risks
- The technological options, its financial, operational, and business requirements
- The views of relevant interested parties

Date: 01/05/18	Program: New eyewash/showers, Chemical mixing		Program #: PRG-02	
OH&S objective: Install two new eyewash/shower units			Project leader: Mike Smith	
Target: Install by June 01, 2018			Estimated completion date: June 01, 2018	
#	Task	Responsibility	Schedule	Complete
1	Select supplier	Mike S.	01/25/18	
2	Determine location	Bob S.	02/01/18	
3	Purchase eyewear/shower units	Mike S.	03/10/18	
4	Install units	Bob S.	05/01/18	
5	Test units	Mike S.	05/10/18	
6	Add to inspection list	Mike S.	05/10/18	

Figure 6.6 Smith Coating Company example program.

To implement the objectives, a program needs to be created to define the responsibilities, timeline, and methods. An example of an OH&S program for the Smith Coating Company is shown in Figure 6.6.

The status of the programs should be tracked and communicated to the employees in a timely manner until the program is completed and the objective is achieved.

Internal Audit Questions

6.2.2 Planning to Achieve OH&S Objectives

How does the organization maintain programs for achieving the OH&S objectives?

Does the organization's program's designate:

- Responsibility and authority for achieving objectives
- The means and time frame by which the OH&S objectives are to be achieved

How are programs supported throughout various levels in the organization?

7
Support

#	ISO 45001:2018	#	OHSAS 18001:2007
7	Support		
7.1	Resources	4.4.1	Resources, roles, responsibility, accountability, and authority
7.2	Competence	4.4.2	Competence, training, and awareness
7.3	Awareness	4.4.2	Competence, training, and awareness
7.4	Communication	4.4.3	Communication, participation, and consultation
7.4.1	General	4.4.3.1	Communication
7.4.2	Internal communication	4.4.3.1	Communication
7.4.3	External communication	4.4.3.1	Communication
7.5	Documented information	4.4.4	Documentation
7.5.1	General	4.4.4	Documentation
7.5.2	**Creating and updating**		NEW
7.5.3	Control of documented information	4.4.4 / 4.5.4	Control of documents / Control of records

---

7.1 Resources

The organization shall define and provide the resources needed for the establishment, implementation, maintenance, and continual improvement of the OH&S management system.

7.1 RESOURCES

Clause 7.1 ("Resources") defines the resources needed to establish, implement, maintain, and continually improve the OH&S management system. The ISO 45001:2018 clauses and subclauses are illustrated in Figure 7.1.

The support and resource clauses of ISO 45001:2018 cover requirements for how the organization will:

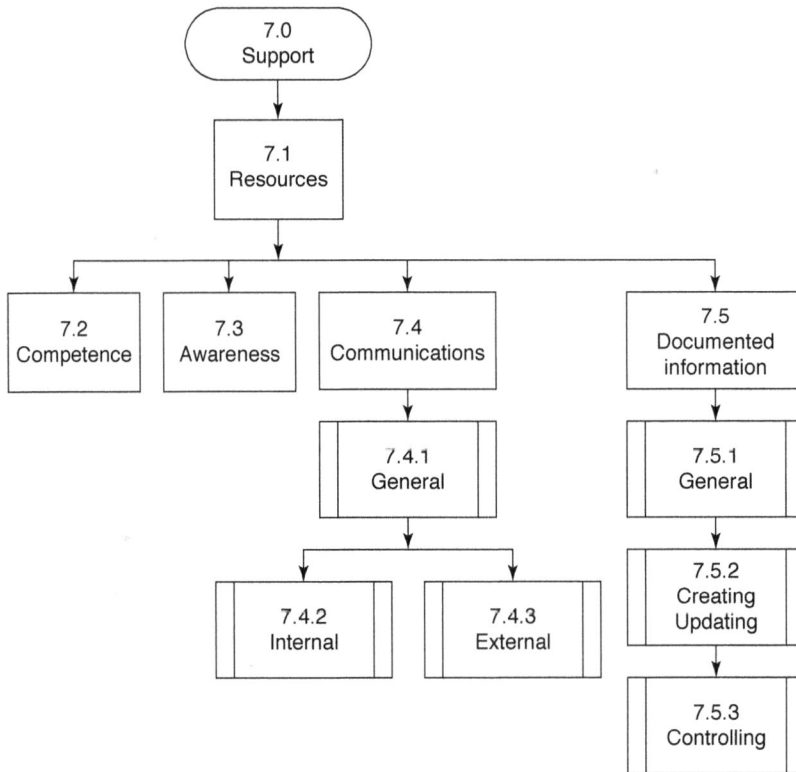

Figure 7.1　Resources: ISO 45001 subclauses.

- Determine the competence of persons doing work under its control

- Make persons doing work under the organization's control aware of the requirements of the OH&S management system and the potential impacts associated with their work

- Plan and implement a process for internal and external communications relevant to the OH&S management system

- Create, update, and control documented information required by the OH&S management system and ISO 45001:2018

7.2 Competence

The organization shall:

- Define the necessary competence of workers that affects or can affect its OH&S performance;

- Ensure that workers are competent (including having the ability to identify hazards) on the basis of appropriate education, training, or experience;

- Where applicable, take actions to ensure that workers acquire and maintain the necessary competence and evaluate the effectiveness of training and of actions taken;

- Retain appropriate records as evidence of competence.

7.2 COMPETENCE

The organization needs to identify the competence, skills, and training to support the OH&S management system. The organization will need to define what jobs or tasks within the scope of OH&S activities require special skills or capabilities. Then the organization will be required to establish job requirements, qualify the employees per the requirements, and provide training as needed. The organization needs to establish a process to qualify the assigned employees, either by witnessing the employees work, testing them, or, in some cases, subscribe to third-party licensing or a certification program. Where job descriptions are used, the organization should provide a record of how and why the employee matched the job's requirements.

The Smith Coating Company has several activities in its OH&S operation requiring qualification or training. They use a training matrix to define training needs by department (Table 7.1). Each training event has the frequency of training or refresher training defined. A record of training for each employee is retained. The company determines how to verify or qualify that employees were trained as planned. In some cases, work instructions can describe the requirements, and the employee can be qualified by an approved witness sign-off. In other cases,

Table 7.1 Smith Coating Company training matrix.

OH&S training	Coating	Mixing	Slitting	Maintenance	Warehouse	Admin.
Accident and incident report	X	X	X	X	X	X
Bladed tools	X		X	X		
Respirators		X		X		
HazCom	X	X	X	X	X	X
Confined space	X	X		X		
Contractor responsibilities				X		X
Emergency rally points	X	X	X	X	X	X
Employee safety handbook	X	X	X	X	X	X
Eye protection	X	X	X	X	X	X
Fall protection	X			X		
Fork truck operation				X	X	
HazCom HMIS labeling	X	X	X	X	X	X
Hoist inspection		X		X		
Housekeeping	X	X	X	X	X	
ISO awareness	X	X	X	X	X	X
LOTO awareness	X	X	X	X	X	
Personal electronics	X		X	X		
PPE filter bags		X				
Static electricity	X	X		X		
Visitor responsibilities						X
Wellness program	X	X	X	X	X	X

Table 7.2   Smith Coating Company training videos.

Training video and quiz	Coating	Mixing	Maintenance	Warehouse	Admin.
Bloodborne pathogens	X	X	X	X	X
Confined space entry	X		X		
Contractor and visitor awareness			X		X
Cranes, chains, slings, and hoists	X	X	X		
Driving safety—street smarts	X	X	X	X	X
Electrical high voltage safety			X		
Flammable liquids	X	X	X		
Fork truck safety—best operating practice			X	X	
Hand safety—injury prevention	X	X	X	X	X
Hazcom—erase the mystery	X	X	X	X	X
Hearing conservation (mandatory)	X	X	X	X	X
LOTO affected	X		X	X	
Respiratory safety		X	X		
Static electricity	X	X	X		

such as maintenance of hoists or fork trucks, external training may be required and certification recorded.

For workers in manufacturing, the work instructions should identify safety-related aspects of the jobs. In the Smith Coating Company, the workers in the chemical mixing department have requirements listed for personal protective equipment (PPE) for eyewear, shield, dust masks, and so forth. All applicable employees need to have chemical right-to-know training, as well as annual refresher courses relating to OSHA and company OH&S procedures. Smith Coating Company uses video training with quizzes to ensure their employees are properly trained as outlined in Table 7.2.

Internal Auditor Questions

7.2 Competence

How does the organization identify training needs associated with its OH&S risks and its OH&S management system?

What are the tasks requiring training in the OH&S management system?

- Lockout/tagout
- Working at heights
- Permissible chemical exposure limits (PEL)
- Personal protective equipment (PPE)
- Confined space entry
- Hazard communication (HazCom)

- Process safety management (PSM)
- Blood-borne pathogens (BBP)
- Powered lift equipment

Describe tasks with an external training and a certification or licensing requirement.

7.3 Awareness

Workers and workers performing tasks on behalf of the organization shall be made aware of:

- The OH&S policy and OH&S objectives;
- Their contribution to the effectiveness of the OH&S management system, including the benefits of improved OH&S performance;
- The implications and potential consequences of not conforming to the OH&S management system requirements;
- Incidents and the outcomes of investigations that are relevant to them;
- Hazards, OH&S risks, and actions determined to be relevant to them;
- The ability to remove themselves from work situations that they believe may present an imminent and serious danger to their life or health and the awareness that they are protected from undue consequences for doing so.

7.3 AWARENESS

Clause 7.3 ("Awareness") overlaps somewhat with clause 7.2 ("Competence") because making employees and others *aware* requires some level of *training*; however, clause 7.3 focuses more on the general understanding of the OH&S management system as opposed to the ability to recognize specific tasks that affect the organization's OH&S performance as described in clause 7.2. Of special importance is making visitors or individuals working at the site aware of the hazards at the site, including the need for the requirement of PPE, such as safety eyewear.

Plantwide or department-level safety meetings should be held at regular intervals to ensure employees are kept up to date on OH&S-related activities, including review of incident investigations. Most manufacturing companies I have visited maintain a safety committee, consisting of a cross-section of company members.

Top management must emphasize that employees need never put themselves in a work situation they consider a danger to their lives or health. The awareness process for people working on behalf of the organization is typically audited by interviewing employees (and on-site contractors). A third-party auditor will expect the employees to have a general understanding of the organization's OH&S policy, how the policy applies to them, and the location of the OH&S policy. Additionally, the auditor would expect the interviewee to have some knowledge of the organization's OH&S objectives and how the employee could support the objectives.

Internal Auditor Questions

7.3 Awareness

How does the organization make persons working under its control aware of the OH&S consequences of their work activities, their behavior, and the OH&S benefits of improved personal performance?

How does the organization make persons working under its control aware of their roles and responsibilities and their importance in achieving conformity to the OH&S policy and procedures?

How does the organization make persons working under its control aware of the potential consequences of departure from specified procedures?

7.4.1 General

The organization shall establish, document, and maintain the process for the internal and external communications relevant to the OH&S management system, including the criteria for the content and timing of OH&S communications, as well as techniques for communicating to contractors and visitors to the workplace and other interested parties.

The organization shall take into account diversity aspects (e.g., gender, language, culture, literacy, disability) when establishing its communication processes.

The organization shall ensure that the views of external interested parties are considered in establishing its communication process.

When establishing its communication process, the organization shall: .

- Take into account its legal requirements and other requirements;
- Ensure that OH&S information to be communicated is consistent with information generated within the OH&S management system and is reliable.

The organization shall respond to relevant communication requests on its OH&S management system.

7.4 COMMUNICATION

7.4.1 General

Clause 7.4.1 provides the overview for the organization's requirements relating to communications relevant to its OH&S management system. This clause outlines the need for the organization to establish a communications procedure for internal and external OH&S communications, including the requirement to retain records of the organization's communications. Of particular importance to the organization's communication process is the clear communication to contractors working on the site of safety requirements. Clause 8 ("Operational Controls") will provide communications options for contractors working on the site. To ensure the information communicated is *reliable* and free from error may require a consideration of close review and approval of OH&S communications.

7.4.2 Internal Communication

The organization shall:

- Internally communicate information relevant to the OH&S management system among the various levels and functions of the organization, including any changes to the OH&S management system, as appropriate;
- Ensure its communication process enables workers to contribute to continual improvement.

7.4.3 External Communication

The organization shall externally communicate information relevant to the OH&S management system as established by the organization's communication process, taking into account its legal requirements and other requirements.

7.4.2–7.4.3 Internal and External Communication

The grid shown in Table 7.3 might be useful in helping to distinguish the intent and conformance evidence among the three clauses: Competence (7.2), Awareness (7.3), and Communications (7.4).

The best practices I've witnessed for internal communications of the OH&S include the use in various plant locations of television monitors scrolling updated information relating to the organization's safety record, OH&S objectives, and performance, including workplace-safety tips.

The intent of external communications is to ensure the organization follows up on communications from neighbors, regulatory agencies, or other interested parties. An example would be a neighbor of the plant complaining about the organization's trucks driving too fast through the neighborhood, thereby endangering children. The organization should respond to the complaint, establish corrections as appropriate, and communicate with the neighbor. When a regulatory agency visits the site, the event should be documented with any follow-up actions defined

---

Table 7.3 Focus for competence, awareness, and communications.

#	Clause	Focus	Objective Evidence
7.2	Competence	Employee/contractor ability to perform tasks within the OH&S	Job descriptions; training records and licenses
7.3	Awareness	Employee understanding of the intent of the OH&S and the objectives	Awareness meeting attendance; employee interviews
7.4.2	Internal communications	Changes in the OH&S; employee contributions to improvement	Postings in the plant; employee interviews
7.4.3	External communications	Ensure follow-up to external communications	Communication logs; compliance reports

and implementation dates noted. A communications log is useful tool to record the complaints and regulatory visits. Personnel charged with responding should be trained for that job.

As part of the organization's external communication process, the organization should record how it will respond to requests by the public (or customers) for information relating to its OH&S program. Will the organization provide the public with a copy of the OH&S policy? Is the policy on the organization's website or other communication link? Who in the organization has the authority to talk to the news media about a serious safety incident at the site?

Internal Auditor Questions

7.4.1–7.4.3 Internal Communication, External Communication

Describe the organization's process for providing internal and external communications relevant to the organization's OH&S management system.

How does the organization provide internal communications among the various levels and functions of the organization relating to OH&S hazards and the OH&S management system?

How does the organization provide internal communications when changes occur in the OH&S management system?

How does the organization ensure its communication process enables workers to contribute to continual improvement?

How does the organization communicate with contractors and other visitors to the workplace?

How does the organization receive, document, and respond to relevant communications from external interested parties?

- Regulatory bodies
- Neighbors or other interested parties

7.5.1 General

The organization's OH&S management system shall include:

- Documentation information required by ISO 45001:2018;
- Documentation information defined by the organization as being necessary for the effectiveness and control of the OH&S management system.

7.5 DOCUMENTED INFORMATION

7.5.1 General

The ISO 45001:2018 standard follows the requirements of Annex SL. Prior to the release of ISO 9001:2015, the ISO-created Annex SL was intended to harmonize all ISO management systems' terminology and formatting. It was designed to make it easier for organizations, which have to comply with more than one management system standard, to manage their documentation. ISO 9001:2015 and ISO 14001:2015 were released using Annex SL formatting.

In Annex SL, the term "documented information" was created to cover the information that had been generally referred to as documents and records. As described by Annex SL, if the organization needs to prepare information and instructions for describing what needs to be done, they are *maintaining* documented information. This information had formerly been described in the ISO terminology as *procedures, work instructions*, and *forms*. If the organization needs to provide information validating performance or results, they are *retaining* documented information. This information was formerly defined as *records*.

Helping several clients update to ISO 9001:2015 and ISO 14001:2015, I found no value in using "documented information" in place of procedures and records. In fact, the new terminology has contributed confusion. OH&S management system records are of extreme importance in validating an organization's efforts to protect the health and safety of its workers. This handbook uses the conventional terminology of procedures and records. There is no requirement to adopt the new terminology.

The overarching principle in documentation should be to formalize what is needed to ensure that users of the documentation have a source for information and instructions that is accurate and timely, providing consistency in managing the business. A goal of the handbook is to assist organizations in managing OH&S management documentation that meets their business needs, while satisfying ISO 45001:2018 requirements.

Internal Auditor Questions

7.5.1 Documentation General

Where are the following documents located?

- The description of the context and scope of the OH&S management system
- The OH&S policy and objectives

How does the organization describe the main processes/elements of the OH&S management system?

How does the organization provide links or references to lower level documentation?

How does the organization decide which elements require a procedure or documented instruction to ensure the effective planning, operation, and control of processes that relate to the management of its OH&S risks?

> ### 7.5.2 Creating and Updating (New Clause)
>
> When creating and updating documentation the organization shall ensure appropriate:
>
> - Identification and description (e.g., a title, date, author, or reference number);
> - Format (e.g., language, software version, graphics) and medium (e.g., paper, electronic);
> - Periodic review and approval for suitability and adequacy.

7.5.2 Creating and Updating

ISO 45001:2018 clause 7.5.2 ("Creating and Updating Documented Information") is more prescriptive than OHSAS 18001:2007. Organizations now required to format their documents (procedures, work instructions, and forms) need to include a title, date, author, or reference number and the type of format (software version, graphics) and whether the medium is paper or electronic. This is good practice, although the forms that become safety records when populated normally contain just a title and revision number or date initiated; the author and format can be recorded elsewhere.

The documents need to be reviewed and approved. In past revisions, the responsibilities for preparation of documents and approval were inconsistently interpreted by various organizations. The procedure describing preparation of documented information should clearly define who will prepare documents (e.g., process owner) and who will approve documents (e.g., safety manager or plant manager or other authority). The best practice is to have a minimum of two employees sign off on each document. If a third-party consultant assists the organization in preparing the documentation, a member of the organization's management needs to be part of the approval process.

The requirements for *Review and approval for suitability and adequacy* are somewhat vague as has been the case for prior ISO revisions. I would suggest the organization establish a *review* process for documentation commensurate with the risks of deviation from employee instructions. The intent of the review process should be to ensure the OH&S documentation (procedures, work instructions, standard operating procedures [SOPs]) matches current practices. Operating personnel may improvise how they perform a task either to improve their efficiency or to save steps: this cannot be allowed without management approval. The internal audit process may be a suitable method of monitoring *documentation versus practice,* provided that audit notes include evidence that work instructions were validated. In other cases, work instructions should be reviewed by the appropriate authority at regular intervals. My suggestion would be to have the organization establish a priority list, ranking the *risk level* of not following work instructions as it relates to potential for an increased safety risk (or a history of injury-prone activities). An example would be failure to use the personal protective equipment required in chemical mixing areas. During audits, I have observed workers transferring chemicals wearing only safety glasses when the work instructions required full face shields. These instructions should be formally reviewed at least annually.

Internal Auditor Questions

7.5.2 Creating and Updating

How does the organization define the process for the identification and description (e.g., a title, date, author, or reference number) for each document?

How does the organization define the format (e.g., language, software version, graphics) and medium (e.g., paper, electronic) for each document?

How does the organization define the process to approve documents for adequacy prior to issue?

7.5.3 Control of Documented Information

Documentation information (OH&S procedures and records) required by the OH&S management system and by ISO 45001:2018 shall be controlled to ensure:

- Documentation is available and suitable for use, where and when needed;
- Documentation is adequately protected from loss of confidentiality, improper use, or loss of integrity.

For the control of documented information, including OH&S records, the organization shall define the following activities as applicable:

- Distribution, access, retrieval, and use;
- Storage and preservation, including preservation of legibility;
- Control of changes (e.g., version control);
- Retention and disposition.

Documents and OH&S records of external origin determined by the organization to be necessary for the planning and operation of the OH&S management system shall be identified, as appropriate, and controlled.

7.5.3 Control of Documented Information

Control of documents requires the organization to ensure procedures and instructions created to inform employees about how to complete their assigned tasks are maintained. In simple terms, any document or note that tells an employee how to do a job should be controlled. Most OH&S documents will be controlled in a formal documentation system as described in clause 7.5.2. Tips sheets or sketches posted on a machine that provide guidance on operating the machine can be considered "controlled" if the area supervisor has initialed and dated the note. This exception-approval process should be documented. Likewise, if temporary deviations of procedures are allowed, the organization's change control procedure should define the allowable conditions, including time limits for temporary deviations.

The organization should ensure documents and records are adequately protected from loss of confidentiality, improper use, or loss of integrity.

Internal Auditor Questions

7.5.3 Control of Documented Information (Procedures, Work Instructions, Forms)

What is the organization's process for changing documents and providing revision control and record of change?

How does the organization ensure relevant versions of applicable documents are available at points of use?

How does the organization review and update procedures and work instructions to ensure they are being used by employees as documented?

What is the process to prevent the unintended use of obsolete documents and to ensure that the documents remain legible and readily identifiable?

What is the process to ensure documents of external origin required for the OH&S management system are identified and their distribution controlled?

OH&S records are an important part of the OH&S management system. In addition to providing evidence of conformance to a specification or requirement, safety records are an integral component when responding to OSHA inspections. The Smith Coating Company OH&S management system records are listed in Table 7.4. An example of an OH&S management system records matrix is shown in Table 7.5.

Table 7.4   Smith Coating Company OH&S records.

Inspections	Employees	OH&S management system
Eyewash/showers	Training	Incidents
Fire extinguishers	Injuries	Management review
Sprinklers		Corrective actions
Fork trucks		Internal audits
Hoists		Compliance audits
Exits		Communications
Ladders		Accidents
Static grounding		JSA
Plant tours		
Regulatory		

Table 7.5   Smith Coating Company OH&S records matrix.

Record title	Form #	Location	Type	Retention	Disposition
OH&S Incident	SF-101	Safety Office	Copy	5 years	Archive
Fire Extinguisher Inspections	SF-102	H drive	E-file	5 years	Archive

Documents of external origin determined by the organization to be necessary for the planning and operation of the OH&S management system, need to be identified, as appropriate, and controlled. Examples of external documents would include OSHA 29 CFR 1910 regulations and supplier equipment manuals. The organization should maintain an external document list for all relevant OH&S management system external documents which defines location, how accessed, and how the documents are kept current with revision-level control process defined.

Internal Auditor Questions

7.5.3 Control of Documented Information (OH&S Records)

How does the organization identify, store, and protect OH&S records required to demonstrate conformity to its OH&S management system?

Where are the records identified, linked to a procedure or work instruction, or listed in a records matrix?

How are the records accessed and where are they stored?

Is the retention time for records defined?

What is the process used to dispose of outdated records?

8

Operation

#	ISO 45001:2018	#	OHSAS 18001:2007
8	Operation	4.4.6	Operational control
8.1	Operational planning and control	4.4	Implementation and operation
8.1.1	General		
8.1.2	Eliminating hazards and reducing OH&S risks	4.3.1	Hazard identification, risk assessment, and determining control
8.1.3	Management of change	4.3.1g, h	Hazard identification, risk assessment, and determining control
8.1.4	Procurement	4.4.6b	Operational control
8.2	Emergency preparedness and response	4.4.7	Emergency preparedness and response

8.1.1 General

The organization shall implement, document, and maintain the processes needed to meet requirements of the OH&S management system and to implement the actions and controls defined during the process used to address risks and opportunities by:

- Establishing criteria for developing the processes;
- Implementing control of the processes in accordance with the criteria;
- Maintaining and retaining records to the extent necessary to have confidence that the processes have been carried out as planned;
- Adapting work techniques to the ability of workers.

At multiemployer workplaces (where there are workers from outside the organization), the organization shall coordinate the relevant parts of the OH&S management system with the other organizations to ensure all workers at the workplace have safe and healthy working conditions.

8.1.2 Eliminating Hazards and Reducing OH&S Risks

The organization shall establish, document, and maintain a process for the elimination of hazards and reduction of OH&S risks considering the following "hierarchy of control" (as appropriate to the risk level of the hazard and associated costs):

- Eliminate the hazard;
- Substitute with less hazardous processes, operations, materials, or equipment;
- Use engineering controls and reorganization of work;
- Use administrative controls, including training;
- Use adequate personal protective equipment.

8.1 OPERATIONAL PLANNING AND CONTROL

8.1.1–8.1.2 General, Eliminating Hazards and Reducing OH&S Risks

ISO 45001:2018 clause 8.1 ("Operational Planning and Control") was written to conform with Annex SL and to align with the ISO 9001:2015 and ISO 14001:2015 standards. In my opinion, this conformance complicates the interpretation of the operational control requirements in the OH&S. The health and safety aspects of manufacturing processes are a *subset* of the manufacturing process; they are very important, but they are not the process. The key processes in OH&S management systems are identifying hazards, reducing risks, and maintaining conformance to workplace legal regulations. There are distinct OH&S processes, such as safety inspections, incident reporting, and emergency planning. Requirements for these processes are defined in other clauses of ISO 45001:2018.

The safety requirements of manufacturing processes, combined with the OH&S processes and clause 8.1 of ISO 45001:2018, can be displayed graphically as shown in Figure 8.1.

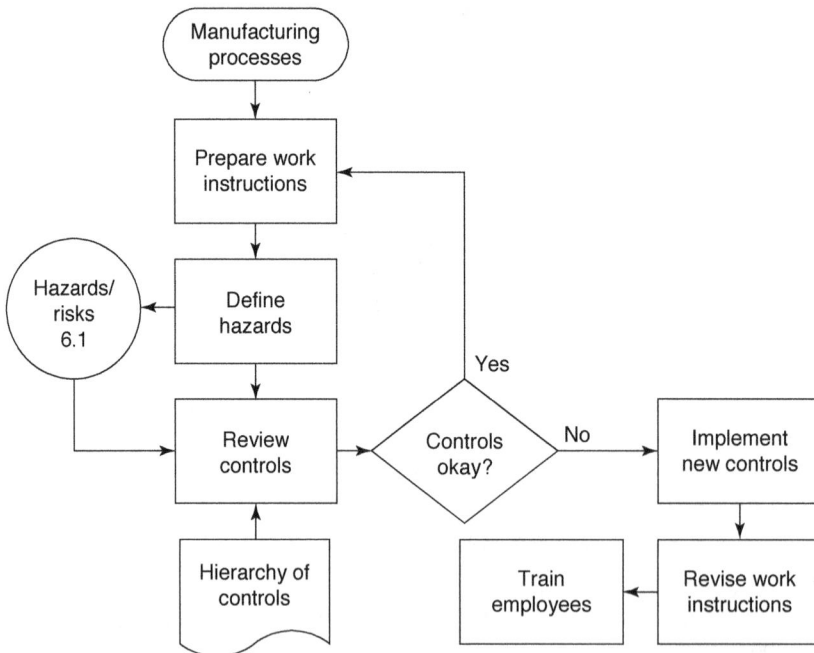

Figure 8.1   Process to establish OH&S work instructions related to manufacturing.

Each manufacturing or support process in the organization will have work instructions describing the tasks. The hazards and risk process as described in Chapter 6 calls for a review of the safety hazards that may be inherent in the task and requires a job safety analysis or similar technique to determine the risks and the appropriate controls to protect the worker from injury, Once the controls are approved or modified, the manufacturing work instruction will be updated, and the affected employees will be trained. Returning to the job safety analysis for the Smith Coating Company from Chapter 6, the JSA can be completed by adding new controls as appropriate. The RPN was calculated as part of the JSA in Chapter 6 and helped prioritize the risks. See Figure 8.2.

After review with the mix area workers, plant engineer, safety manager, and plant manager, a proposal was presented and approved to purchase and install a new hoist system to lift bags to the mezzanine and allow their positioning over the tank. To remind workers to wear PPE, large "safe practice" posters were added to the work area, and a new training video was obtained. Plant engineering will arrange to have air quality sampled this year. The workers requested research for PPE gloves that allow easier use of utility knives. Other controls were accepted as sufficient.

The application of the "hierarchy of controls" was considered when applying OH&S controls:

- Eliminate the hazard (highest)

- Substitute with less hazardous processes, operations, materials, or equipment

- Use engineering controls and reorganization of work

- Use administrative controls, including training

- Use adequate personal protective equipment (lowest)

With respect to the task of lifting chemical packages to the mezzanine, it was agreed that a better hoisting system would provide more protection for the workers by avoiding back strain. After Smith Coating Company had the air quality in

JSA Worksheet				
Job: Chemical Mixing		**Prepared by: Mike**		**Date: Jan. 12, 2017**
Task	**Potential Hazard**	**Existing Controls**	**RPN**	**New controls?**
Lifting chemical packages	Back or body injury	Training hoist	60	Install new hoist with boom arm
Dispensing materials	Chemical burn	PPE: Gloves, safety glasses	48	Add posters to area; new training DVD
	Material inhalation	PPE: Dust masks	24	Conduct air test
	Hand cut	PPE: Safety knives, gloves	12	Research more flexible gloves
	Eye injury	PPE: Safety glasses	16	Audit area more frequently
Working on mezzanine	Fall	Guardrails	12	Continue current
	Injury to coworker	Safety helmet	16	Continue current

Figure 8.2 Smith Coating Company JSA worksheet controls analysis.

the chemical mix area analyzed, the company decided to study the need for an enhanced exhaust filtration system.

I added the phrase "as appropriate to the risk level of the hazard and associated costs" to the phrasing of clause 8.1.2 ("Eliminating Hazards and Reducing OH&S Risks") because a third-party auditor does not have the authority to require and organization to implement the highest-ranked control.

There are cost-benefit considerations that need to be evaluated before an organization selects a control option. For example, in a plant with a noise level requiring personal protection equipment (ear plugs), the cost of eliminating the noise hazard by installing noise-reduction panels could be prohibitive. The auditor should expect the organization to have a process to *review* the hierarchy of hazards and record the rationale for the option the organization selects.

The proper application of a JSA will satisfy ISO 45001:2018 clauses 6 and 8.1.2 ("Eliminating Hazards and Reducing OH&S Risks") requirements and is a good application of plan-do-check-act (PDCA).

To address the clause 8.1.1 ("General") requirements relating to situations of multiemployer (multiworkers) workplaces, where there are workers from outside the organization, a clear definition of responsibilities and maintenance of operational controls is necessary as a starting point. There are two common situations that can occur: Company "A" leases a section of the site to Company "B" or Company A leases a section of a site from Company B, where Company A is the ISO 45001:2018 certified site. As described in clause 4.3 ("Determining the Scope of the OH&S Management System"), there need to be agreements between the two companies.

In the case where the organization (Company A) leases the property from Company B, the organization has the responsibility to ensure its processes or activities do not have an adverse impact on workplace safety of the personnel or property of Company B. The renting organization and the owner of the property need to coordinate communication on fire safety, evacuation drills, and other worker safety issues.

Likewise, when Company B rents space from Company A, the ISO 45001:2018 certified organization, Company A needs to spell out the OH&S requirements to be observed between the two companies. Examples include notification of fire alarm testing and evacuation protocols, restrictions of storage of flammable materials, use of pedestrian walkways in areas with fork truck safety, and PPE requirements when crossing common areas.

The responsibilities, restrictions, and agreements for multiemployee workplaces should be documented in the organization's OH&S management system manual or similar document. In some cases, signed agreements may be required to ensure clear communications and implementation of safety issues relating to all individuals employed at the site or complex. The responsibility for reporting accidents required by OSHA 29 CFR 1910.1904.7 form 300 needs to be defined. An organization housing employees from another company would be wise to seek legal advice to understand potential liabilities.

Multiemployee/employer sites present a high potential for accidents or injuries if responsibilities and communications are not clearly defined and controlled. When I was auditing a multiemployee location, I would delve deeply into the two-company arrangements and audit the implementation actions, including the testing of the plans. I was at a large multiemployee site when the fire alarm sounded. The engineering company leasing a section of the organization's site did not hold an evacuation, even though the alarm sounded in the engineering office. An interesting discussion ensued between the plant manager and the engineers.

> **Internal Auditor Questions**
>
> **8.1.1 Operational Planning and Control**
>
> *How does the organization define the controls in the OH&S management system relating to managing and controlling risks with respect to:*
>
> - Manufacturing
> - Maintenance
> - Chemical handling
> - Plant support equipment
> - Hoists, ladders, powered trucks
> - Laboratories
> - Warehouse
> - Servicing
>
> **8.1.2 Eliminating Hazards and Reducing OH&S Risks**
>
> *How does the organization use the "hierarchy of controls" to reduce OH&S risks and establish best-control practices? Provide examples.*

8.1.3 Management of Change

The organization shall establish and document a process for the implementation and control of planned temporary and permanent changes that impact OH&S performance including:

- New products, services, and processes, or changes to existing products, services, and processes including:
    - Workplace locations and surroundings;
    - Work organization;
    - Working conditions;
    - Equipment;
    - Work force.
- Changes to legal requirements and other requirements;
- Changes in knowledge or information about hazards and OH&S risks;
- Developments in knowledge and technology.

The organization shall review the consequences of unintended changes, taking action to mitigate any adverse effects, as necessary.

8.1.3 Management of Change

OHSAS 18001 had requirements for change control in clauses 4.3.1g, h ("Hazard Identification, Risk Assessment and Determining Controls"). ISO 45001:2018 provides a new management of change clause as part of the alignment with Annex

SL. Several clauses of ISO 45001:2018 also include requirements for control change: clause 6.1 ("Actions to Address Risks and Opportunities"), 7.4.2 ("Internal Communications"), 7.5.3 ("Control of Documented Information"), and 9.3 ("Management Review"). An effective change control process is central to the success of all management systems.

In an OH&S management system, the change control process can be managed by the organization's quality management, or the OH&S management system can create a standalone process. As described under clause 6.1.2 ("Hazard Identification and Assessment of Risks and Opportunities"), changes in the OH&S management system can present a risk to the safety of workers.

A change control process will include a cross-functional sign-off on changes in the manufacturing or servicing processes and the impact of those changes on their OH&S. The ECN (engineering change notice) or similar system will require that the appropriate individuals review and approve changes to ensure the organization's workers are protected from injury when changes are implemented. Changes that can present new safety risks to workers include machinery, processing, and new materials. Many organizations require that new capital requests be approved by the organization's safety department before new machinery or equipment can be installed to ensure the appropriate safety-related aspects (guards, electrical standards, noise, etc.) are included with the new equipment. Before releasing new machines to production, a safety department sign-off should be required.

New chemicals should not be allowed to be brought on site before the affected workers are made aware of the potential hazards as defined in the appropriate Safety Data Sheets (SDS). In my OHSAS 18001 (and ISO 14001) auditing experience, SDS management was frequently deficient. Readers of this handbook might consider auditing their plants to assess the SDS process. Select ten chemicals, record the product's identification number, and look for the corresponding SDS. I suspect that many of the audits would reveal at least one missing SDS, often because a container of lubricant, epoxy paint, or cleaning fluid was brought into the plant by an engineer or mechanic without going through the purchasing department.

A challenging requirement is presented by clause 8.1.3: "The organization shall review the consequences of *unintended* changes, taking action to mitigate any adverse effects, as necessary." The organization's emergency planning process may need to include *unintended changes* in addition to fires and bad weather.

Internal Auditor Questions

8.1.3 Management of Change

How does the organization manage changes that can affect the OH&S management system?

How are changes in the following processes controlled to prevent risks in the OH&S management system?

- Documentation
- Process or equipment
- Facilities
- Materials
- Workers

8.1.4 Procurement

8.1.4.1 General

The organization shall establish, document, and maintain a process to control the procurement of products and services in order to ensure their conformity to the organization's OH&S management system.

8.1.4.2 Contractors

The organization shall coordinate its procurement process with its contractors to identify hazards and to assess and control the OH&S risks arising from the:

- Contractors' activities and operations that impact the organization;
- Organization's activities and operations that impact the contractors' workers;
- Contractors' activities and operations that impact other interested parties in the workplace.

The organization shall ensure that the requirements of its OH&S management system are met by contractors and their workers. The organization's procurement process shall define and apply occupational health and safety criteria for the selection of contractors. Records of acknowledgements and agreements with contractors shall be retained.

8.1.4 Procurement

OHSAS 18001:2007 included requirement clause 4.4.6 ("Operational Control"): For those operations and activities, the organization shall implement and maintain controls relating to purchased goods, equipment, and services.

ISO 45001:2018 requires the same control, using the terms *procurement of product and services*. As described under clause 8.1.3 ("Management of Change"), purchase orders for equipment and materials need to be reviewed prior to approval to ensure potential safety issues are addressed. While most companies embrace this concept, there are opportunities for discrepancies. Third party auditors will test the effectiveness of the organization's control of purchased items by reviewing a sample of purchase orders and looking for clarity in safety-related specifications.

8.1.4.2 Contractors

Control of noncompany individuals working at the organization's site presents a challenge to the organization's OH&S both in preventing the safety risks the nonemployee can present to the organization's employees as well the noncompany employee's risk of being injured while working at the site. There are four categories of noncompany individuals that may come onto the organization's site (Table 8.1).

Visitors to the site to attend a meeting or similar function should be required to sign in and out of the site. When visitors enter the manufacturing areas, they should be accompanied by a company escort and comply with the PPE requirement of the OH&S management system.

Temporary workers are persons hired on a part-time basis to replace or supplement the organization's work force; they should receive the same OH&S management system training and indoctrination as the organization's own workers that perform the same tasks (clause 7.2 applies). In big organizations, there is often a

Table 8.1 Reasons for nonemployee individuals to be at the organization's site.

Category	Type of work
Visitors	Escort individuals attending meetings or similar activities
Temporary workers	Perform tasks to replace the organization's employees
Contractors on site	Perform maintenance or construction or other services at the organization's site
Suppliers or vendors	Produce and deliver materials or services to the organization.

large contingent of temporary workers; the temporary workers' training records may reside with the temporary help agency. The organization needs to ensure that the agency understands and conveys the organization's safety requirements effectively. A third-party auditor will ask to review the temporary workers' training records and may interview temporary workers at the site during the audit.

When the organization hires a *contractor* (a person working under its control) to provide services, such as maintenance, cleaning, painting, or construction, both the construction company's management and the workers at the site need to conform to the organization's OH&S safety requirements. In many organizations, contractors pose a high OH&S risk potential due to the nature of their work (welding, working at heights). There are several options available to provide indoctrination or training for contractors. At a minimum, the contractor needs to sign in and out of the site each day. If there is an emergency evacuation at the site, the organization will want to account for all individuals at the site. A common communication/orientation/training technique involves having contractors read and sign the OH&S requirements to indicate their understanding and agreement. Requirements should be defined for:

- Personal protection equipment (PPE)

- Permits for use of open flames

- Lockout of energized equipment

- Approval of chemicals

- Working at heights

In sites with hazardous manufacturing processes—chemical plants or metals mining operations—contractors may be required to attend a safety training module and view a plant safety video. During audits at high hazard companies, I was often required to attend a safety training session before I could start my audit. A few years back, I audited an oil rig platform in the Gulf of Mexico, 150 miles off the coast of Louisiana. I spent four hours, along with rig construction workers, being advised of the rig's OH&S requirements, including the location and deployment of life rafts.

Suppliers or vendors provide materials or services to the organization, such as removing waste or delivering supplies. The organization may want to treat certain suppliers the same as visitors, depending on the activity. Waste removal company employees may require access to the plant; OH&S training requirements may then be the same as those for contractors.

Internal Auditor Questions

8.1.4 Procurement

How does the organization control the following processes in the OH&S management system relating to:

- Purchased goods, equipment and services
- Contractors
- Visitors

How does the organization ensure contractors working at the organization's site are aware of the organization's OH&S requirements?

8.1.4.3 Outsourcing

The organization shall ensure that outsourced functions and processes are controlled. The organization shall ensure that its outsourcing arrangements are consistent with legal requirements and other requirements and with achieving the intended outcomes of the OH&S management system. The type and degree of control to be applied to these functions and processes shall be defined within the OH&S management system. Records of acknowledgement and agreements with outsourced partners shall be retained.

8.1.4.3 Outsourcing

The multiemployee situation described previously can result in a situation requiring "outsourcing" controls. If the employees from the company renting space at the certified organization's site are providing products or services that are not part of the organization's supply chain—an independent business—then the OH&S controls are as described previously in clause 8.1 ("Operational Planning and Control"). If the second company working at the certified organization's site produces materials or services to support the certified organization's manufacturing, that is "outsourcing." A company producing printed books may outsource processes at its site. The printing company may hire another company with expertise in making the ink used in the organization's printing presses to produce the ink at the site near the presses rather than at the ink company's site.

There will be situations created by the other company's workers that could impact the health and safety of the workers of the parent organization. The ink company's workers will need to be made aware of OH&S requirements when crossing through the organization's buildings (wearing safety glasses, fork truck safety). A third-party auditor will want to see evidence of the OH&S agreements between the certified organization and the outsourced workers to ensure that all employees at the site have a safe workplace.

I would interview the outsourced workers to assess their awareness of the certified organization's fire safety rules, as well as of their own policies regarding safe handling of chemicals, static grounding, spill protection, and so forth. During an audit at a printing company, I was rebuffed by the outsourced company's manager because he felt his company's operations were outside the scope of my audit. This difference of opinion resulted in a meeting with the certified organization's purchasing manager and the ink manager. My audit of the ink company continued.

When the outsourced process is performed at the supplier's site, the certified organization does not have direct control over the supplier's OH&S performance other than selecting suppliers who maintain a safe workplace. I was responsible for procuring materials for many years when I worked at Polaroid. Part of the supplier selection process was to visit the supplier's plant and tour the operation. Rejecting a supplier due to poor housekeeping and safety deficiencies was common. I am pleased to see that organizations such as bluesign® (Chapter 6) require suppliers in the textile manufacturing pipeline to maintain a safe workplace.

Internal Auditor Questions

8.1.4.3 Outsourcing

How does the organization define the OH&S controls relating to outsourced processes, suppliers, and contractors working at the organization's site?

- Cleaning services
- Waste removal
- Maintenance
- Construction
- Other

When workers from another company are working at the organization's site, how does the organization ensure the OH&S requirements are maintained to protect the safety of both the organization's workers and the other company's workers?

8.2 Emergency Preparedness and Response

The organization shall establish, document, and maintain a process needed to prepare for and respond to potential emergency situations as identified in the hazards identification including:

- Establishing a planned response to emergency situations, including the provision of first aid;
- Providing training for the planned response;
- Periodically testing and exercising the planned response capability;
- Evaluating performance and, as necessary, revising the planned response, including after testing and, in particular, after the occurrence of an emergency situation;
- Communicating and providing relevant information to all workers about their duties and responsibilities;
- Communicating relevant information to contractors, visitors, emergency response services, government authorities, and, as appropriate, the local community;
- Taking into account the needs and capabilities of all relevant interested parties and ensuring their involvement, as appropriate, in the development of the planned response.

8.2 EMERGENCY PREPAREDNESS AND RESPONSE

There is some overlap for organizations relating to planning and responding to emergencies for *safety* and *environmental* incidents. It is up to the organization to determine how it will design and implement the emergency preparedness and response plan. From the ISO 45001:2018 perspective, the emergency planning requirements focus on the protection of workers from injury or ill health when an incident occurs. A fire in a plant will be a personnel and plant *safety* incident; however, the incident will also have an environmental impact due to possible air and water contamination from sprinkler discharge interacting with materials and chemical and volatile emissions during burning. To avoid redundancies, many organizations combine their environmental health and safety (EHS) emergency planning and preparedness into an integrated plan.

The plan should cover emergency situations and accidents that could occur at the site, including fire, chemical release, explosion, severe weather, terrorists, and sudden illness of an employee. The written procedures should describe the plan for dealing with each potential incident as well as the implementation and testing of the plan. Questions for consideration when establishing the emergency preparedness and response plan for fire or explosion might include:

- Has the necessary support equipment (sprinklers, spill kits, fire extinguishers, etc.) been purchased, installed, and maintained?

- What employee training requirements/records are required?

- Is there an emergency response team?

- What follow-up or corrective action must occur as a result of an incident?

- Has the organization coordinated its plan with local agencies (fire department, regional emergency responders)?

- Should the safety emergency planning procedures be combined with the environmental emergency planning procedures?

The organization should assess weather conditions that could create an emergency situation at the site that could endanger the employees and should plan accordingly. Tornadoes and storms should be included depending on the location of the site and its weather history. Tornadoes are common in many areas of the United States, and the organization should establish safe areas for assembly and hold drills.

Other emergency actions, such as responding to an injured employee requiring immediate medical attention in order to save a life or limb should be planned as appropriate to the organization's operations. The procedures for requesting aid from local resources (fire department, emergency medical agencies) should be part of the plan. It is common for local authorities to have copies of the organization's emergency plans. Local emergency support agencies often visit sites to assist with emergency testing.

Defibrillators are often located at a company. Qualification of the organization's medical response team is of paramount importance, as is maintenance of the medical equipment. When I audit at sites that maintain first aid kits or other medical apparatus, I verify that the first aid kits are maintained and that first responders are properly trained. I have been disappointed to observe that the first aid kits are often mostly empty or a dust protection face mask, without its protective packaging is setting on a dirty shelf.

The organization should test the emergency procedures where *practicable*, meaning "able to be done" or "feasible." The inference in ISO 45001:2018 is that it may not be feasible to simulate, or test, an actual chemical spill or a fire or explosion; however, the response activities of trained employees and all employees can be evaluated through drills, and so forth. Fire alarms need to be tested and are required by local fire department regulations as well as by insurance companies. The best practices I have observed with testing of emergency preparedness include an analysis of the potential emergency incidents that might occur at the site (a history of incidents can assist the study) and development of a strategy to address the risk of occurrence. In one year, a mock chemical spill might be simulated; at another time a full evacuation drill with execution of emergency apparatus could be planned. Records of drills, as well as of actual emergency incidents, need to be retained, and correction of deficiencies observed during the testing or incident should be entered into the organization's corrective action process.

In all cases, all work shifts should be included in the plans. Most plant engineers or safety engineers reading this section will tell you the emergency "ghosts" seem to prefer working after sundown!

Internal Auditor Questions

8.2 Emergency Preparedness and Response

How has the organization documented the emergency planning to prevent or mitigate associated adverse OH&S consequences?

How does the organization's emergency plan consider the needs of relevant interested parties, such as emergency services and neighbors?

How has the organization outlined its response to:

- A fire
- Liquid spills
- Unintended release of gases
- Worker injury or illness
- Bad weather events
- Bomb threat, terrorist

How are emergency procedures reviewed and revised following the occurrence of accidents or emergency situations?

How has coordination with the local fire department and other authorities been considered (if applicable)?

How does the organization test the emergency response plans? How frequently?

If testing is not done, how does the organization ensure the emergency responses will be effective?

How are deficiencies discovered during testing responded to and resolved?

How does the organization ensure that medical support apparatus is maintained (if applicable)?

How does the organization ensure the emergency support devices are maintained (sprinklers, fire pumps, alarms, etc.)?

9
Performance Evaluation

#	ISO 45001:2018	#	OHSAS 18001:2007
9	Performance evaluation	4.5	Checking (title only)
9.1	Monitoring, measurement, analysis and evaluation	4.5.1	Performance measurement and monitoring
9.1.1	General		
9.1.2	Evaluation of compliance	4.5.2	Evaluation of compliance
9.2	Internal audit	4.5.5	Internal audit
9.2.2	Internal audit program	4.5.5	Internal audit
9.3	Management review	4.6	Management review

9.1.1 General

The organization shall establish and document a process for monitoring, measuring, analyzing, and evaluating performance of the OH&S management system to assess the effectiveness of the OH&S management system.

The process shall include, where applicable, the methods, criteria, and frequency of monitoring.

The organization shall define what needs to be monitored and measured, including:

- The extent to which legal requirements and other requirements are fulfilled;
- Its activities and operations relating to identified hazards, risks, and opportunities;
- Progress towards achievement of the organization's OH&S objectives;
- Effectiveness of operational and other controls.

Calibration: The organization shall ensure that monitoring and measuring equipment relating to the OH&S is calibrated or verified as applicable to relevant legal requirements and is used and maintained as specified by the organization.

The organization shall retain appropriate records as evidence of the results of calibration or verification of measuring equipment.

9.1 MONITORING, MEASUREMENT, ANALYSIS, AND EVALUATION

9.1.1 General

The performance evaluation clause is the "check" step in the PDCA cycle (plan-do-check-act). Graphically, performance evaluation has four subsets (Figure 9.1): monitoring and measurement (objectives, operating controls, and OH&S performance); evaluation of compliance; internal audit; and management review.

The organization can employ various techniques to provide evidence of its monitoring and measurement commitments. The management review notes can provide this evidence. Table 9.1 is an outline of a possible monitoring and measurement approach.

A third-party auditor will review the organization's monitoring techniques for each OH&S process to assess both the process used and the results. The management review notes will be a good way for the organization to summarize OH&S performance. The auditor may observe that the injury rates are rising. If the organization has not effectively applied hazard and risk analyses, a nonconformance may be issued, but not against clause 9.1.1 ("Performance"). The nonconformance would relate to clause 6.1 ("Actions to Address Risks and Opportunities"). If the organization does not have an effective process to monitor worker injuries, the nonconformance could apply to clause 9.1.1 ("Performance"). To monitor the effectiveness of operational controls, the compliance audit described below can be used.

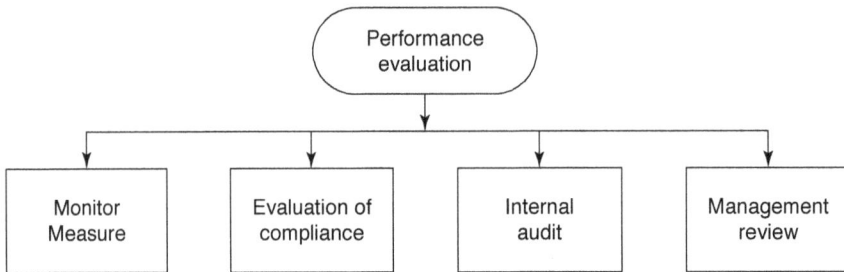

Figure 9.1 Subclauses of performance evaluation.

Table 9.1 Options for monitoring OH&S processes.

Process	Monitoring technique	Evidence
Legal requirements and other requirements	Compliance audit	Compliance audit report
Hazards, risks, and opportunities	Job safety analysis	Injury metrics
OH&S objectives	Management review	Management review notes
Operational controls	Internal audit; compliance audit	Internal audit notes; compliance audit notes

The devices in the OH&S that support evidence that the organization is meeting its compliance obligations or those devices established to protect workers from injury or ill health should be calibrated or verified at specified intervals. Some examples:

- Vapor analyzers: monitor a wide variety of gases to prevent fires or explosions

- Static grounding cables: eliminate sparking potential and trigger for fire

- Noise monitors: measure noise levels

Additionally, there may be medical devices or kits that need to be monitored. Defibrillators are often found in manufacturing plants to provide emergency medical support for a worker experiencing a heart attack: Defibrillators require maintenance, validation, and a battery charger; training in its proper use is also needed. First aid kits should be inspected at specific intervals to ensure that they are adequately supplied.

Internal Auditor Questions

9.1.1 General

What are the measures relating to the organization's OH&S?

- Accident rate
- Lost time accident rate
- Incident reports
- Near miss incidents

How does the organization monitor the extent to which its OH&S objectives are met?

How does the organization monitor the effectiveness of controls for health as well as for safety?

What are the proactive measures of performance that monitor conformance with the OH&S programs, controls, and operational criteria?

How does the organization use the results of monitoring and measurement to facilitate subsequent corrective action analysis?

How does the organization calibrate or verify and maintain the equipment applicable to its OH&S?

- Noise
- Particulate matter
- Chemical
- Gas levels

9.1.2 Evaluation of Compliance

The organization shall establish, document, and maintain a process for evaluating compliance with legal requirements and other requirements applicable to the organization's OH&S.

The organization shall:

- Define the frequency and methods for the evaluation of compliance;
- Evaluate compliance results and take action, if needed, to maintain compliance;
- Maintain knowledge and understanding of its compliance status with legal requirements and other requirements;
- Retain records of the implementation of the compliance program, audit results, and corrective actions.

9.1.2 Evaluation of Compliance

There are two steps involved in conducting an audit of an organization's legal and other requirements: the legal list review and a plant tour.

The baseline for the compliance audit should be the legal and other lists from this handbook's Section 6.1.3. Each OH&S legal requirement should be checked to see if any changes have occurred since the last review. A review of the OH&S legal inspection records that may be required include:

- Fire system protection (extinguishers, sprinklers)
- Eyewash/showers

A plant audit should be conducted, starting with a review of the operational controls defined in Chapter 8. The work instructions or similar documents will indicate where inspections or other records are required during the plant audit. During the plant tour, potential safety hazards or violations of the organization's legal requirements should be noted and recorded in the organization's corrective action process (Chapter 10). A compliance audit checklist can be used during the plant tour. Some of the items that may be included on the list[1]:

Work Areas

- Are the Material Safety Data Sheets placed in locations accessible to all employees?
- Are hazards identified by signs and tags?
- Have all trucks, forklifts and other equipment been inspected and maintained?
- Are lockouts or tag out procedures in place and followed?
- Is ventilation equipment working effectively?
- Is the fume and dust collection hood working effectively?
- Are the safety showers and eyewash stations in the proper locations?

---

[1] From the Canadian Centre for Occupational Health and Safety.

Fire Emergency Procedures

- Is there a clear fire response plan posted for each work area?

- Do all workers know the plan?

- Are drills held regularly?

- Are fire extinguishers chosen for the type of fire most likely to occur in that area?

- Are there enough extinguishers present to do the job?

- Are extinguisher locations conspicuously marked?

- Are extinguishers properly mounted and easily accessible?

- Are all extinguishers fully charged and operable?

- Are special-purpose extinguishers clearly marked?

Means of Exit

- Are there enough exits to allow prompt escape?

- Do employees have easy access to exits?

- Are exits unlocked to allow egress?

- Are exits clearly marked?

- Are exits and exit routes equipped with emergency lighting?

Warehouse and Shipping

- Are dock platforms, bumpers, stairs, and steps in good condition?

- Are light fixtures in good condition?

- Are all work areas clean and free of debris?

- Are stored materials properly stacked and spaced?

While the items listed on the compliance checklist may not have a direct connection to the organization's OH&S legal requirements, a list can be an efficient way to combine compliance auditing with monitoring of OH&S operational controls required by clause 9.1.1.

Frequency of Compliance Audits

ISO 45001:2018 requires the organization to establish the frequency at which compliance audits will be conducted. For a company seeking registration to ISO 45001:2018, a baseline compliance audit is required before the registrar can recommend certification. An existing compliance report can be used provided it was performed within the previous year and presented a thorough review of the organization's compliance obligations. Each organization needs to understand the adherent risk in its operations relating to the impact on the OH&S program before deciding on the interval between compliance audits. Large organizations, with more than one site will often have qualified compliance auditors on the corporate staff who will conduct compliance audits at each plant. More frequently, organizations will employ a third-party consultant to conduct the compliance audit every three to five years. In either case, during the intervening years, it is recommended that a compliance audit be conducted each year, using a qualified member of the organization's staff.

Agreement should be established between a third-party ISO 45001:2018 auditor and the organization as how the auditor will report issues that could result in nonconformity with its legal requirements. Normally, the auditor should not record potential OSHA violations. ISO auditors are not OSHA experts and should refrain from making judgments regarding OSHA requirements. I verbally inform the organization when I detect a potential OSHA violation and do not record the defect.

Review of internal compliance audits by ISO auditors falls under *client-attorney privilege,* a legal concept in the United States that protects certain communications between a client and the attorney and keeps those communications confidential. An organization being audited often cites client-attorney privilege when the auditor requests to review the organization's internal compliance audit report. The organization's concern is that there may be an OSHA violation exposed by the internal compliance auditor which is not yet public knowledge. The ISO 45001:2018 auditor should review with the registrar how compliance confidentiality issues should be addressed. In my experience, if an organization cites client-attorney privilege, the third-party auditor need only establish that there is a process for compliance auditing and that the corrections are in place.

Internal Auditor Questions

9.1.2 Evaluation of Compliance

How does the organization audit the applicable legal requirements?

Where is the compliance plan documented? Is audit frequency specified?

Who conducts compliance audits and how are they qualified?

How are audit deficiencies responded to and resolved?

How does the organization review compliance with "other" OH&S requirements relating to customers, industry, or corporate?

9.2 Internal Audit

9.2.1 General

The organization shall conduct internal audits at planned intervals to determine whether the OH&S management system conforms to the organization's own requirements for its OH&S management system and to the requirements of ISO 45001:2018 and shall determine that the audits are effectively implemented and maintained.

9.2.2 Internal Audit Program

The organization shall:

- Establish, document, and maintain an audit program which includes the frequency, methods, responsibilities, consultation, planning requirements, and reporting, taking into consideration the importance of the processes concerned and the results of previous audits;

- Define the audit criteria and the scope of each audit;
- Select auditors and conduct audits to ensure objectivity and impartiality of the audit process;
- Ensure that the results of the audits are reported to relevant managers, workers, and workers' representatives, as applicable, and to other relevant interested parties;
- Take action to address nonconformities and continually improve its OH&S performance;
- Retain records as evidence of the implementation of the audit program and maintain audit results.

9.2 INTERNAL AUDIT

Many organizations seeking or holding registration to ISO 45001:2018 presently maintain certification to the quality management system ISO 9001 or ISO 14001. For those organizations, the quality internal audit procedure can be extended to cover the requirements of ISO 45001. Quality auditors can be trained to the requirements of ISO 45001:2018. ISO 14001 trained auditors can be very effective OH&S auditors because the standards have much in common. Many organizations combine or integrate their EMS and OH&S management system internal audits.

In establishing an internal audit process for the environmental management system, the company has several questions to address:

- What is the schedule or audit plan?
- How is the schedule established?
- Have all OH&S MS processes/clauses been audited?
- How is audit evidence obtained and recorded?
- Has an internal OH&S MS audit team been established?
- Have the auditors been trained/qualified?
- Are audits conducted according to schedule?
- Are the follow-up actions performed and management reports issued on a timely basis?

For an organization seeking registration to ISO 45001:2018, evidence should be provided that indicates the organization conducted an internal audit with respect to all clauses in ISO 45001:2018. The internal audit results should provide information on whether the OH&S management system conforms to the requirements of this international standard. Additionally, the organization needs to demonstrate that the organization conforms to its own requirements for its OH&S management system.

My recommendation for most organizations is to conduct full OH&S management system audits each year. The organization should consider the risks associated with the processes within the OH&S management system and allocate more audit time to the manufacturing processes with highest risks or a high injury-rate history. A sample audit plan for the Smith Coating Company is outlined in Figure 9.2.

The processes in the Smith Coating Company relating to the ISO 45001:2018 clauses are diagrammed. While the OH&S management system does not lend itself to *process* audits, it is sufficient when conducting internal audits to review documents, records, and communications while auditing according to a manufacturing clause. The Smith Coating Company conducted audits in chemical mixing every six months as the injury risks were high. It is good practice to commit auditing resources commensurate with the OH&S risks.

Auditors must perform an objective and impartial audit. An internal auditor from the operational control process should not be assigned to audit his/her own process. The individual assigned responsibility and authority to manage the OH&S management system needs to be judicious on whether they personally get too involved in providing internal audits for clauses they have responsibility to manage.

The organization needs to maintain a report of the results of the internal audit, including a summary report defining how the audit was conducted, issues raised (nonconformances and opportunities for improvements), and follow-up activities defined. Nonconformances should be entered into the organization's corrective action process. Opportunities for improvement (OFIs) should be addressed by the organization, with follow-up responses documented.

Process-based internal audits have been used effectively in the quality management system and can also be used to audit the operating controls in the OH&S management systems. See the example illustrated in Figure 9.3.

Internal Auditor Questions

9.2 Internal Audit

How does the organization plan and schedule internal audits of the OH&S management system? How often are internal audits conducted?

Is the audit plan linked to the clauses of ISO 45001:2018?

How are the internal auditors trained and qualified to perform OH&S internal audits?

How does the organization ensure the internal audits are conducted with objectivity and impartiality?

What methods are used by the internal auditors to collect information regarding the OH&S processes, procedures, instructions, and requirements relating to the OH&S management system?

How are discrepancies or nonconformities (findings) discovered when conducting internal audits of the OH&S management system recorded?

Process	Impact	Frequency	Scope	Leadership	Planning	Competence	Communications	Documents	Operational	Emergency	Performance	Improvement
Management	M	12	x	x	x	x	x		x		x	x
Purchasing	L	18				x		x	x			
Chemical mix	H	6			x	x	x	x	x	x		
Coating	M	12			x	x	x	x	x	x		
Converting	M	12			x	x	x	x	x	x		
Shipping	M	12			x	x	x	x	x	x		
Facilities	M	12			x	x	x	x	x	x		
H.R.	M	12				x	x	x				
OH&S	H	6			x	x	x	x	x	x	x	x

Figure 9.2 OH&S process-based internal audit plan.

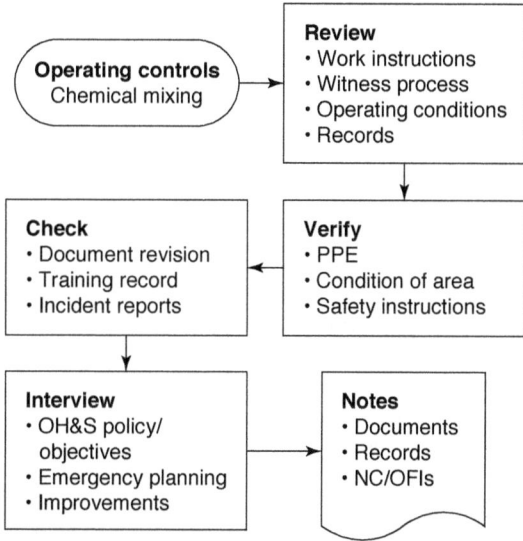

Figure 9.3 Process-based internal audit example.

9.3 Management Review

Top management shall review the organization's OH&S management system, at planned intervals, to ensure its continuing suitability, adequacy, and effectiveness.

The management review shall include:

- The status of actions from previous management reviews;
- Changes in external and internal issues that are relevant to the OH&S management system including:
  - ◦ The needs and expectations of interested parties;
  - ◦ Legal requirements and other requirements;
  - ◦ Risks and opportunities.
- The extent to which the OH&S policy and the OH&S objectives have been met
- Information on the OH&S performance, including trends in:
  - ◦ Incidents, nonconformities, corrective actions, and continual improvement;
  - ◦ Monitoring and measurement results;
  - ◦ Results of evaluation of compliance with legal requirements and other requirements;
  - ◦ Audit results;
  - ◦ Consultation and participation of workers;
  - ◦ Risks and opportunities.
- Adequacy of resources for maintaining an effective OH&S management system;
- Relevant communication with interested parties;
- Opportunities for continual improvement.

The outputs of the management review shall include decisions relating to:

- Continuing suitability, adequacy, and effectiveness of the OH&S management system in achieving its intended outcomes;
- Continual improvement opportunities;
- Any need for changes to the OH&S management system;
- Resources needed;
- Actions needed;
- Opportunities to improve integration of the OH&S management system with other business processes;
- Any implications for the strategic direction of the organization.

Top management shall communicate the relevant outputs of management reviews to workers and workers' representatives, as applicable. The organization shall maintain records as evidence of the results of management reviews.

9.3 MANAGEMENT REVIEW

The organization has several options relating to reporting the status of the OH&S management system. The review meeting can be incorporated into the organization's integrated business meeting along with the environmental and quality management review or other business management meetings. Whatever the format, the agenda of the OH&S management system is fairly straightforward and prescriptive; each agenda topic needs to be addressed during the frequency cycle established in the organization's plan. At a minimum, the OH&S management system should be reviewed annually by the organization's top management staff.

Consistent with the requirement of ISO 45001:2018 clause 5.1 ("Leadership and Commitment"), *ensuring the integration of the OH&S management system requirements into the organization's business processes,* the top management of the organization should both attend, and fully participate in, the management review meetings. The emphasis is on top management's strong involvement in the OH&S. Many OHSAS 18001:2007–certified organizations have integrated safety and health management reviews into their business model and strategy. I have audited many companies where the OH&S performance metrics are woven into the business plan. The key performance indicators (KPIs) assigned to quality, environmental, and business parameters also include the safety metrics of accident rates, near misses, and employee wellness programs.

During the meeting, top management should assess the *suitability, adequacy,* and *effectiveness* of the OH&S management system. "Suitability" questions whether the OH&S management system is *adequate* to address the organization's current processes and occupational health and safety hazards and risks; suitability looks at what tasks the organization's workers need to perform. If the organization adds new manufacturing or service activities, does the OH&S management system needs to be adjusted? "Adequacy" of the OH&S management system asks whether the organization satisfies the requirements of ISO 45001:2018. "Effectiveness" examines whether the organization is achieving the desired results and objectives. When reviewing the management system, management should provide a summary statement as to the suitability, adequacy, and effectiveness of the OH&S management system, highlighting any gaps that exist and any management actions (and resources) that are required to set the commitments back on course.

Internal Auditor Questions

9.3 Management Review

How frequently does the organization review suitability, adequacy, and effectiveness of its OH&S management system?

Does the organization's management review cover the following agenda items:

- Results of internal audits
- Results of compliance audits
- Update of hazards and risks
- Results of worker participation and consultation
- Communications from external interested parties, including complaints
- The OH&S performance of the organization and the extent to which OH&S objectives have been met
- Status of incident investigations and corrective actions
- Follow-up actions from previous management reviews
- Changing circumstances, including developments in legal and other requirements relating to OH&S
- Recommendations for improvement

How does the organization record decisions regarding changes made during OH&S Management Review meetings?

- OH&S policy
- OH&S objectives and targets

What evidence supports the organization's commitment to continual improvement of the OH&S management system?

How are relevant outputs from management review made available for communication and consultation with employees?

10

Improvement

#	ISO 45001:2018	#	OHSAS 18001:2007
10.1	General	4.1 4.2	General requirements OH&S policy
10.2	Nonconformity and corrective action	4.5.3 4.5.3.1 4.5.3.2	Incident investigation, nonconformity, corrective action, and preventive action (title only) Incident investigation Nonconformity, corrective and preventive action
10.3	Continual improvement	4.1 4.6	General requirements Management review

10.1 General

The organization shall define opportunities for improvement and implement necessary actions to prevent work-related injury and ill health to workers and to achieve the intended outcomes of its OH&S management system.

10.2 Incident, Nonconformity, and Corrective Action

The organization shall establish, document, and maintain a corrective action process to include reporting, investigating, and taking appropriate action to correct and control OH&S incidents and nonconformities in a timely manner.

The organization, with the appropriate participation of workers and the involvement of other relevant interested parties, shall evaluate the need for corrective action to eliminate the root causes of the incident or nonconformity, to ensure that it does not recur or occur elsewhere by:

- Investigating the incident or reviewing the nonconformity;
- Defining the cause(s) of the incident or nonconformity;
- Examining if similar incidents have occurred or if nonconformities exist or could occur.

The organization shall review its defined OH&S risks and hazards to evaluate if application of the corrective action process can reduce or eliminate the hazards and risks.

The organization shall review the effectiveness of any action taken, including corrective action, to make changes to the OH&S management system as appropriate. Corrective actions shall be appropriate to the effects or potential effects of the incidents or nonconformities encountered.

The organization shall maintain records as evidence of the description of the incidents or nonconformities and any subsequent action(s) taken, including the result(s) of any action and corrective action and review of the effectiveness of the action(s) taken.

The organization shall communicate records of any corrective action(s) to relevant workers and workers' representatives, if applicable, and to other relevant interested parties.

10.3 Continual Improvement

The organization shall continually improve the suitability, adequacy, and effectiveness of the OH&S management system by:

- Promoting a culture that supports an OH&S management system;
- Promoting the participation of workers in implementing actions for the continual improvement of the OH&S management system;
- Communicating the relevant results of continual improvement to workers and, where they exist, to workers' representatives;
- Maintaining records as evidence of continual improvement.

Clause 10 ("Improvement") requires the organization to establish and maintain processes to detect and correct errors and make improvements in the OH&S management system. In addition to ensuring that the organization complies with its OH&S legal obligations, the ISO 45001:2018 standard requires the organization to analyze and improve its OH&S performance. OHSAS 18001:2007 includes clause 4.5.3 ("Nonconformity, Corrective Action and Preventive Action"), but there is no direct requirement for *continual improvement*. Note: ISO 45001:2018 removes the preventive action requirement since one of the key purposes of an OH&S management system is to act as a preventive tool; the risk analysis clause of ISO 45001:2018 is a form of preventive action.

The hazards and risk analysis process, properly implemented (clause 6.1), will reduce workplace injuries, *improving* the health and safety of the organization's workers. Additionally, clause 6.2 requires the organization to establish OH&S objectives and programs to *improve* OH&S performance. The grid in Table 10.1 may be useful in summarizing the OH&S improvements and defining evidence needed to support conformance.

The organization can use the practice of third-party auditing to the ISO 45001:2018 standard to reduce worker injuries by implementing a strong hazards and risk analysis process, applying effective controls, and providing effective training to its workers. To sustain the improvements, the organization will have to create a work culture that makes workplace safety a priority. There are programs available for assisting companies wanting to make a major leap in safety performance.

Table 10.1 OH&S improvement sources and evidence of conformance.

Subclause	Improvement source	Evidence
6.2.2 OH&S programs	• Performance against OH&S objectives • Trend charts related to injury rates • New PPE or safety equipment	• Management review notes • Improvement team meeting notes • Employee interviews
	Correction source	
10.2 Incident, nonconformity, and corrective action	• OH&S incidents • Emergency drills • Compliance audits • Regulatory inspections • Neighbor complaints • Plant tours • Internal audits	• Audit notes, findings • Tour notes • Employee suggestions • Regulator citations • Communications log

OSHA's Voluntary Protection Program (VPP) has helped many organizations make a major reduction in injuries for more than 30 years. To qualify for VPP, applicants must have in place an effective safety and health management system that meets rigorous performance-based criteria. Certification to ISO 45001:2018 can help build the baseline for entry into VPP. Appendix B provides an overview of VPP. VPP is often used in high-safety-risk manufacturing companies: paper mills, metal processors, and chemical manufacturers. There are also programs available for organizations in lower-safety-risk industries.

OSHA established the Safety & Health Achievement Recognition Program (SHARP). The program recognizes small business employers (<250 employees) who have used OSHA's On-site Consultation Program and operate an exemplary injury and illness prevention program (https://www.osha.gov/dcsp/small business/sharp.html). The site includes some great OH&S success stories for small companies.

I observed an innovative program, while auditing in Canada a few years ago, called "SafeTrack." The company that provides the program is "SafeStart" (http://www.safestart.com). It offers a wide variety of safety training (I do not have any connection to the company). One program focuses on human-error-prevention training to reduce injuries. One of the techniques used by the SafeTrack program is peer observation of a worker performing a task to evaluate the potential for injury. The observer is trained to look for certain behaviors or actions that might place the worker at risk of injury and to evaluate the worker using the observation card (Figure 10.1). I think the "observation card" technique could be useful to many organizations to enhance their hazard and risk analysis and to support worker participation.

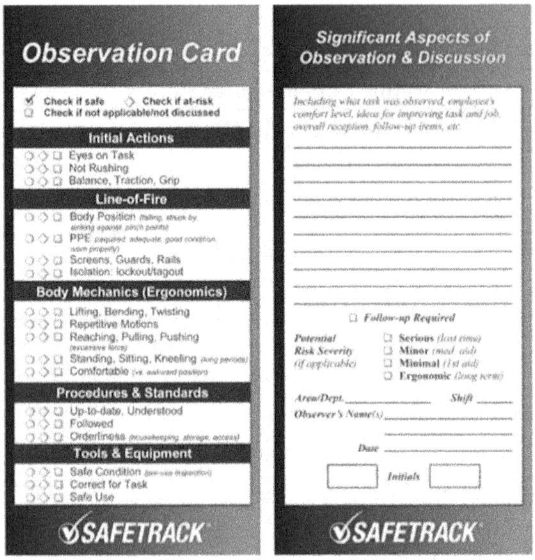

Figure 10.1   SafeTrack observation card.

Internal Auditor Questions

10.1 and 10.3 Continual Improvement

What is the evidence to indicate the organization has supported initiatives to reduce injuries and ill health?

- Injury trends
- Worker participation

Describe programs or initiatives employed by the organization to improve the performance of the OH&S management system.

Most companies, whether they have a formal quality management system or not, will have a corrective action process. For more than 25 years, the ISO 9001 quality management system has promulgated corrective action initiatives, which, in my opinion, have made a major contribution to improving manufacturing product quality and services. In applying the corrective action process based on ISO 45001:2018, there are several requirements, some similar to quality requirements, others unique to occupational health and safety controls.

The sources of correction actions in the OH&S management system include:

- Accidents resulting in injury to workers
- Findings in compliance audits or internal audits
- Deficiencies discovered during emergency drills
- Deficiencies discovered during plant inspections

Plant inspection: Feb. 2, 2017	Responsible	Repair	Follow-up	Date Closed
Fire extinguisher blocked by table in shipping dept.	John	Removed	Notify shipping supervisor	2/3/17
Guardrail broken on mezzanine in mix area	Bob	Issued emergency work order.	Bob will prepare Corrective Action	Open
15-foot ladder not secured in machine room	Bill	Removed and chained to wall	Add to machine room weekly meeting notes as reminder	2/5/17

Figure 10.2   Plant inspection log of OH&S issues.

There are occasions when a formal, multifunction corrective action with cause analysis, effectiveness monitoring, and so forth, are appropriate and situations when a "find-and-fix" approach can be effective. During a plant safety tour, several minor deficiencies might be observed. In these cases, rather than enter these items into the corrective action program, the issue could be corrected, recorded, and closed in situ (Figure 10.2).

The log would be reviewed by the safety manager to ensure that follow-up actions are completed. When defective items are repeated, then a formal nonconformance/corrective action may be issued. In the case where the situation requires the issuance of a corrective action, the action should not only correct the problem but also prompt an analysis of the situation to determine how to prevent recurrence of the issue. In an OH&S corrective action, the actions should include: correct the situation, provide an analysis of the cause, and provide correction for the cause. An example of a corrective action would be:

Description of nonconformance: During a plant safety inspection, two machine guards were not in place on machine number 1.

Correction: Reinstalled guards.

Root cause: New machine operator not properly trained.

Correction for cause: Provide training for new operator.

To ensure corrections resolve the issues and avoid recurrence of the same deficiency, the organization needs to review the effectiveness of any corrective action taken and make changes to the OH&S management system as necessary. In the above example, the root cause analysis may have been incomplete. Unfortunately in safety-related nonconformances, lack of training is frequently the cause of the discrepancy. The organization would want to determine if the training process is adequate and make adjustments as necessary. The organization may decide that worker removal of machine guards will result in disciplinary actions to reinforce the seriousness of the offense.

To protect worker privacy, the organization will want to report accidents that result in injury to a worker separately from the corrective action process.

Third party auditors will devote considerable audit time reviewing the organization's corrective actions and improvement activities. When an auditor notes a discrepancy—say, the fire alarm could not be heard in all areas of the plant during a drill or incident—then the expectation is that the organization will respond with corrections in a timely fashion.

Internal Auditor Questions

10.2 Incident, Nonconformity, and Corrective Action

How does the organization identify and correct nonconformities to mitigate the OH&S consequences of the nonconformity?

- Cause identified and corrected
- Correction for cause identified and corrected to avoid the recurrence of the incident
- The effectiveness of corrective actions reviewed

How does the organization evaluate the need for actions to prevent nonconformities and implement appropriate actions designed to prevent nonconformities:

- Accidents
- Plant inspections
- Results of audits
- Results of drills or emergency situations

How does the organization record and communicate the results of corrective actions to the employees?

How does the organization initiate new controls or risk assessment when the corrective action identifies new or changed hazards?

11

Benefiting from ISO 45001:2018 without Certification

Organizations can improve the health and well-being of their employees by conforming to requirements of ISO 45001:2018 without seeking third-party certification. Using guidances provided in previous chapters of the handbook, an organization can develop a health and safety (H&S) management system by addressing the sections that are key to managing workplace safety. The core sections of the H&S management system requirements include:

1. Health and safety policy

2. Worker training and participation

3. Hazard and risk analysis

4. Legal and other regulations

5. Health and safety controls

6. Emergency planning

7. Management system and compliance auditing

8. Health and safety improvement programs

9. Incident investigations and corrective actions

10. Health and safety reporting

Each of the ten sections has overarching requirements that can assist an organization in conducting a self-assessment or "gap" analysis. Once the analysis is completed and the gaps determined, the organization can use this handbook to close the gaps. Ideally, at some point, a third-party or objective member from the organization can audit the H&S management system. For multisite organizations, the safety manager from one site could conduct the audit at a sister plant and vice versa. The core requirements of a health and safety management system are shown in Table 11.1.

Based on the organization's need for control, the ISO 45001:2018 requirements for scope, leadership, documentation, and communications can be included in the appropriate ten health and safety sections. Expanded requirements for each H&S section are included in the H&S checklists. A CD included with this handbook contains a template of the checklist (Figure 11.1).

Table 11.1 Core requirements of a health and safety management system.

#	Section	Core requirement
1	Health and safety management commitment	Define management's commitment to prevent work-related injury and ill health to workers.
2	Worker training and participation	Define processes and programs to provide safety-related training and include workers participation in identifying hazards and risks and in improving workplace safety.
3	Hazard and risk analysis	Define the process of identifying workplace hazards and mitigation of associated risks.
4	Legal and other regulations	Define the health and safety regulations related to the organization's activities and facilities.
5	Health and safety controls	Define the controls utilized to protect workers from injury and ensure that regulated activities conform to requirements.
6	Emergency planning	Establish, implement, and test plans to respond to an emergency
7	Management system and compliance auditing	Ensure the organization's H&S management system commitments and compliance obligations are met
8	Health and safety improvement programs	Develop and implement programs to improve workplace safety and health
9	Incident investigations and corrective actions	Establish process to investigate safety incidents and provide corrective actions
10	Health and safety reporting	Communicate the performance of the Health & Safety management system.

Company:		
Auditor:	Auditee:	
Section 1: Health and Safety Management Commitment		
Requirement: *Define management's commitment to prevent work-related injury and ill health to workers.*		Y/N
Has management defined its H&S policy or mission to prevent work-related injury or ill health? Describe:		
Has management communicated its H&S policy to workers and others under its control? Explain how:		
Is there evidence of management's support to the H&S management system? Provide examples:		

Figure 11.1 Sample health and safety audit form.

Does management provide resources, training necessary to support the H&S management system? Provide examples:	
Has management assigned responsibilities and provided authorizations necessary to manage the H&S management system? Explain how responsibilities are defined:	

Section 2: Worker Training and Participation	
Requirement: *Define processes and programs to provide safety-related training and include workers participation in identifying hazards and risks and improving workplace safety.*	Y/N
Has management established a process to define the necessary competence of workers that affects the OH&S MS? Define the process:	
Are workers involved in defining hazards in their work? Describe process:	
Does management ask workers for input on improving the safety of the workplace? Describe process:	

Section 3: Hazard and Risk Analysis	
Requirement: *Define the process to identify workplace hazards and mitigation of associated risks.*	Y/N
Has management established a process to define and address the hazards and risks in the workplace? Describe the process:	
Were the workers involved in identifying the hazards in tasks they perform? Describe how:	
Were all manufacturing or servicing processes included in identifying risks? Confirm:	
Were the current controls evaluated as to how effective they were in reducing risk of injury due to the hazards? Describe process:	
Was an action plan established to improve controls to reduce the risks? Describe with examples:	

Figure 11.1   Sample health and safety audit form. *(continued)*

Section 4: Legal and Other Regulations	
Requirement: *Define the health and safety regulations related to the organization's activities or facilities.*	Y/N

Has management defined the health and safety regulations that relate to the organization's activities or facilities?
 	
    Activity   *Available*
    Injury recording
    Servicing machines
    Lockout/tagout
    Machine guarding
    Working at heights
    PPE
    Noise protection
    Tank entry
    Chemical exposure
    Fire safety	

Does management have knowledge of the safety legal regulations related to these activities? Check each applicable activity and note if copy of regulation available:	
Does management have a process for knowing when regulations change? Describe process:	
Section 5: Health and Safety Concerns	
Requirement: *Define the controls utilized to protect workers from injury and ensure regulated activities conform to requirements.*	Y/N
Are controls in place to ensure the regulated activities conform to requirements? Describe process:	
Are there instructions available for workers describing cautions or requirements for equipment required to protect worker's health and safety? Describe how instructions are communicated:	
Is there a process to ensure workers are protected when processes or equipment are changed? Describe process:	
Are visitors and contractors oriented to the organization's health and safety before working at site? Describe:	
Is there a process to ensure purchased materials or outsourced tasks conform to the organization's health and safety requirements? Describe process:	

Figure 11.1 Sample health and safety audit form. *(continued)*

Section 6: Emergency Planning	
Requirement: *Establish, implement, and test plans to respond to an emergency.*	Y/N
Has management defined the situations that could require response to protect the organization's workers and workplace? Define situations:	
Has management prepared a plan to describe the emergency preparedness and planning process? Define plan:	
Has management provided appropriate training and equipment to support the response to an emergency? Describe actions:	
Does management test the plan at some frequency? Describe tests conducted:	
Are local authorities involved in the emergency planning? Describe:	
Section 7: Management System and Compliance Auditing	
Requirement: *Ensure the organization's H&S management system commitments and compliance obligations are met.*	Y/N
Has management established a process to verify its H&S management systems commitments are maintained as planned? Describe how verified:	
Has management established a process to verify its H&S legal obligations are in conformance? Describe how confirmed:	
Section 8: Health and Safety Improvement Programs	
Requirement: *Develop and implement programs to improve workplace safety and health.*	Y/N
Has management initiated and supported activities to make the workplace safer? Explain with examples:	
Are the workers involved in H&S workplace improvements? Explain with examples:	
Does management review the safety performance, injury metrics to support need for new equipment resources? Provide examples:	

Figure 11.1   Sample health and safety audit form. *(continued)*

Section 9: Incident Investigations and Corrective Actions	
Requirement: *Establish process to investigate safety incidents and provide appropriate corrective actions.*	Y/N
Has management established a process to investigate H&S incidents and provide corrections? Describe process:	
Does the corrective action process include investigation of the cause of the incident and actions to prevent recurrence? Describe process:	
Does management communicate the findings and causes of H&S incidents to workers? Define process:	
Section 10: Health and Safety Reporting	
Requirement: *Communicate the performance of the health and safety management system.*	Y/N
Does management communicate the H&S performance to the organization? Describe the reporting process:	
Does management's reporting on the H&S performance include incident metrics and progress on improvement activities? Describe:	

Summary: Describe actions to conform to requirements.			
	Section	**Conforming?**	**Actions**
1	Health and Safety Policy		
2	Worker Training and Participation		
3	Hazard and Risk Analysis		
4	Legal and Other Regulations		
5	Health and Safety Controls		
6	Emergency Planning		
7	Management System and Compliance Auditing		
8	Health and Safety Improvement Programs		
9	Incident Investigations and Corrective Actions		
10	Health and Safety Reporting		

Figure 11.1   Sample health and safety audit form. *(continued)*

12

ISO 45001:2018 Interpretation Guidance

This handbook is the third in a series I have written for publication by the ASQ Quality Press. The ISO 14001:2015 and ISO 9001:2015 implementation handbooks were published in 2016 and 2017, respectively. In preparing the first two books, I had difficulty providing clarity for several clauses due to the new structure Annex SL, particularly around the new terminology for documents and records. In some clauses in this book, I used the prior OHSAS 18001:2007 formatting to help explain the requirements. In my opinion, Annex SL has created unnecessary confusion in its description of the requirements of ISO 45001:2018. The US technical advisory group (TAG) to the project committee, ISO PC283 (charged with developing ISO 45001:2018), approved the often difficult-to-interpret clauses.

This chapter will describe where the new OH&S standard could have been formatted and composed better. ISO 45001:2018 includes excessive indexing, confusing cross-referencing between clauses, and redundancies. In this handbook, I have paraphrased the clauses into straightforward, clearly stated requirements.

BACKGROUND TO ANNEX SL

Prior to issuing ISO 9001 and ISO 14001 with the 2015 revisions, the Technical Management Board of ISO created Annex SL. It was designed to harmonize all ISO management system terminology and formatting, making it easier for organizations to comply with more than one management system standard. Annex SL has ten high-level clauses:

Clause 1: Scope

Clause 2: Normative references

Clause 3: Terms and definitions

Clause 4: Context of the organization

Clause 5: Leadership

Clause 6: Planning

Clause 7: Support

Clause 8: Operation

Clause 9: Performance evaluation

Clause 10: Improvement

I have conducted audits at several organizations with multiple management systems: ISO 9001, ISO 14001, and OHSAS 18001. I have also conducted internal auditor training for organizations on all three standards. During the audits and the training, I found it efficient to have the clauses common to the three standards covered only once. The requirements for document and record control, corrective actions, internal audits, and management review are very similar for the three standards. The competence, awareness, communications, and organizational responsibilities requirements have some commonalities, but these need to be addressed specifically within the context of the management system. The requirements for planning and operational controls for quality, environmental, and safety management systems are distinctly different. The requirement created by Annex SL to force each ISO standard to align with common terminology and formatting has made the process of defining the requirements for planning and controlling processes in ISO 9001, ISO 14001, and ISO 45001 less clear. My concerns are outlined below.

Clause 6.1 Is Confusing, Contains Redundancies, and Is Poorly Formatted

6.1 Actions to Address Risks and Opportunities

6.1.1 General

When planning for the OH&S management system, the organization shall consider the issues referred to in 4.1 (context) and the requirements referred to in 4.2 (interested parties) and 4.3 (the scope of its OH&S management system) and determine the risks and opportunities that need to be addressed to:

a) Give assurance that the OH&S management system can achieve its intended outcome(s);

b) Prevent or reduce undesired effects;

c) Achieve continual improvement.

When determining the risks and opportunities to the OH&S management system and its intended outcomes that need to be addressed, the organization shall take into account:

- Hazards (see 6.1.2.1);
- OH&S risks and other risks (see 6.1.2.2);
- OH&S opportunities and other opportunities (see 6.1.2.3);
- Legal requirements and other requirements (see 6.1.3).

The organization, in its planning process(es), shall determine and assess the risks and opportunities that are relevant to the intended outcomes of the OH&S management system associated with changes in the organization, its processes, or the OH&S management system. In the case of planned changes, permanent or temporary, this assessment shall be undertaken before the change is implemented (see 8.1.3).

The organization shall maintain documented information on:

- Risks and opportunities;

> • The process(es) and actions needed to determine and address its risks and opportunities (see 6.1.2 to 6.1.4) to the extent necessary to have confidence that they are carried out as planned.

Cross-referencing subclauses within the same clause and also referencing other separate clauses of the standard make the requirements of the "Actions to Address Risks and Opportunities" difficult to sort out. Additionally, indexing requirements down four levels is helpful only to an auditor who wants to advise the client, "You are not conforming to clause 6.1.2 sublevel a." Many other clauses of ISO 45001:2018 have multiple "shall" requirements with minimum indexing and cross-referencing. I described the requirements for clause 6.1.1 in the handbook using only two levels and bullet points. The over indexing is a weakness in ISO 9001:2015 and ISO 14001:2015 also, in my opinion.

The quality and environmental standards, ISO 9001:2008 and ISO 14001:2004, issued before adoption of Annex SL contained only one level of indexing (4.2.4a) and was cross-referenced only to highlight the need for records retention. In OHSAS 18001:2007, the clauses had minimal indexing and cross-referencing and were much easier to audit against.

Clause 6.1.4 Has the Cross-Referencing and Indexing Issues but Also Duplicates Requirements from Other Clauses

---

6.1.4 Planning Action

The organization shall plan:

a) Actions to:
   - Address these risks and opportunities (see 6.1.2.2 and 6.1.2.3);
   - Address legal requirements and other requirements (see 6.1.3);
   - Prepare for, and respond to, emergency situations (see 8.2).

b) How to:
   - Integrate the actions into its OH&S management system processes or other business processes and implement them;
   - Evaluate the effectiveness of these actions.

The organization shall take into account the hierarchy of controls (see 8.1.2) and outputs from the OH&S management system when planning to take action.

When planning its actions, the organization shall consider best practices, technological options, and financial, operational, and business requirements.

An understanding and response to the requirements of clause 6.1.1 ("Actions to Address Risks and Opportunities") would also allow an organization be in conformance to this clause 6.1.4 ("Planning Action").

The organization shall plan actions to address legal requirements and other requirements that are more clearly stated in clause 6.1.3 ("Determination of Legal Requirements and Other Requirements").

The organization shall establish, implement, and maintain a process to determine and have access to up-to-date legal requirements and other requirements that are applicable to its hazards, OH&S risks, and OH&S management system.

A proper response to the requirements of clause 6.1.3 will include *planning actions* to address the legal actions. Clause 6.1.4 ("Planning Action") is mostly redundant. The requirement to consider best practices, technological options, and financial, operational, and business requirements should be in clause 6.2.1 ("OH&S Objectives"), consistent with OHSAS 18001:2007 and ISO 14001:2004. Moving "consideration of best practices, technological options, and financial, operational, and business requirements" from the requirements of setting objectives to planning actions is an artifact of Annex SL insistence on management system consistency and adds confusion to the interpretation of the requirements of clause 6.1. The reference to "hierarchy of controls" is also redundant because as the hierarchy of controls is a key requirement in clause 8.1.2 ("Eliminating Hazards and Reducing OH&S Risks"). This handbook provides guidance on responding to these requirements in the clause where the application is most directly related.

Terminology: Documented Information

Under Annex SL, a new term, *documented information*, was created to describe what was formerly *documents and records*. As described by Annex SL, if the organization needs to prepare information and instructions for describing what needs to be done, it is *maintaining* "documented information." "Information and instructions" had formerly been described in the ISO terminology as procedures, work instructions, SOPs, and forms. If the organization needs to provide information validating performance or results, it is *retaining* "documented information," which was formerly defined as "records."

Quality, environmental, and safety records have been an important component of manufacturing and service companies for many decades. Any effort to obfuscate, or diminish the importance of, management system records is not helpful, in my opinion. Quality records are often a key component in resolving product performance disputes and lawsuits. Environmental and employee safety records can be instrumental in assigning financial penalties and can sometimes be admitted as evidence in criminal cases. This handbook uses the traditional terminology.

The clients I have assisted in responding to the new standards have maintained the traditional terminology for documents and records and have successfully upgraded to the 2015 standards for ISO 9001 and ISO 14001. In his book *Understanding the New ISO Management System Requirements* (London: The British Standards Institute, 2014), Dr. David Brewer describes the reason for changing the terminology was for ISO to adapt to modern technology. He and the Technical Management Board of ISO were concerned that if a company today used a web page, the web page could contain both records and procedures, so ISO decided to use a single item to cover both documents and records. In my opinion, Annex SL changed the universally accepted 30-year-old terminology of documents and records to satisfy the very few companies who might conduct their communications on the internet.

Inconsistent Guidance about What Should Be Documented

Under guidance from Annex SL, each of the three "new" standards for management system standards provides inconsistent or vague guidance on what should be documented. There is no requirement cited in 8.1.3 Management of change that relates to "documented information." Accidents and injuries often occur due to the lack of change management. I would strongly suggest that the *change process* include a documented procedure with records of deviation activities retained. Several other clauses, procurement, contractors, and calibration, do not clearly define a requirement for documentation or record retention. In this handbook, I have reworded the ambiguous documentation requirements to specify requirements for documented procedures and retention of records for the majority of clauses.

Prescriptive Requirements

Management system requirements should clearly define *what shall be done* but not *how to satisfy the requirements*. The wording of clause 8.1.2 is "prescriptive," in my opinion.

8.1.2 Eliminating Hazards and Reducing OH&S Risks

The organization shall establish, implement, and maintain a process for the elimination of hazards and the reduction of OH&S risks using the following "hierarchy of controls":

a) Eliminate the hazard;

b) Substitute with less hazardous processes, operations, materials, or equipment;

c) Use engineering controls and reorganization of work;

d) Use administrative controls, including training;

e) Use adequate personal protective equipment.

NOTE: In many countries, legal requirements and other requirements include the provision of personal protective equipment (PPE) to workers at no cost.

The clause, as worded, implies that the organization is *required* to use the hierarchy of controls, implementing the *most effective* control techniques. While most experienced third-party auditors would interpret the wording as a consideration—and the organization would be in conformance if it provided evidence of *considering* the hierarchy of controls when deciding on actions to address the identified hazard. Some auditors, however, would read the wording literally, expecting the organization to implement controls that would eliminate the hazard, disregarding the cost impact on the organization.

There are many organizations that have situations where employees are exposed to high levels of noise. The cost of engineering fixes can be prohibitive. The guiding principle of third-party auditing is that an ISO auditor cannot prescribe or provide consultation on how the audited organization should address or satisfy a requirement. Use of adequate personnel hearing protection can be an appropriate control. (If the workers build a case indicating the need for a better control, the appropriate legal agency [OSHA] will help resolve the issue rather than an ISO auditor or registrar.) The previous OHSAS 18001:2007 standard includes a nonprescriptive requirement: "consideration shall he given to reducing the risks according to the following hierarchy."

In this handbook, I reworded the clause to reflect more clearly the intention of the clause and make it consistent with OHSAS 18001:2007.

The "note" attached to this clause is interesting. While notes in a management standard are not auditable—and usually only provide clarity or examples—the suggestion that auditors follow a trail to be sure the organization is living up to its legal obligation to supply free safety shoes or other personnel protection equipment to workers is also somewhat "prescriptive." I have removed the note from the handbook. If a client of mine were found nonconforming by an auditor for not supplying free safety shoes to workers, I would suggest the auditor consider the potential consequences of getting involved in an organization's legal requirements. There are several notes included in the standard that are problematic, in my opinion.

Inclusion of Prescriptive Notes in the Standards

Dr. David Brewer, author of *Understanding the New ISO Management System Requirements* (London: The British Standards Institute, 2014), describes notes added to a management system as follows:

> A note in an ISO management system is intended to assist readers, to understand the requirement. It does not modify the requirement or imply that a particular way of meeting the requirement is itself a requirement. A sure test of one's understanding of the note is that the requirement should not change if the note is ignored.

A note in the ISO clause should not provide the organization with advice or options on how to satisfy the requirement, or what the third-party auditor can accept as conformance to the requirement. Some examples of misapplied notes in ISO 45001 follow.

ISO 45001 Clause 5.4, "Consultation and Participation of Workers"

Note 2: Obstacles and barriers can include failure to respond to worker inputs or suggestions, language illiteracy, barriers or reprisals or threats of reprisals, and policies or practices that discourage or penalize worker participation.

This note is quite problematic because it suggests a third-party auditor should get involved in a possible workers and management dispute relating to company policy. The auditor can be easily set up by a troubled worker.

ISO 45001 Clause 5.4, "Consultation and Participation of Workers"

Note 4: It is recognized that the provision of training at no cost to workers and the provision of training during working hours, where possible, can remove significant barriers to worker participation.

A management system standard should not advise an organization on how to spend its money.

ISO 45001 Clause 8.1.2, "Eliminating Hazards and Reducing OH&S Risks"

Note: In many countries, legal requirements and other requirements include the requirement that personal protective equipment ("PPE") is provided at no cost to workers.

A third party auditor in the United States should stay clear of informing the management of the organization that they are violating the law by not providing free safety shoes or safety glasses to employees. I wouldn't approach a legal issue in any country.

ISO 45001 Clause 8.1.4.2, "Contractors" and 8.1.4.3, "Outsourcing"

Note: It can be helpful to include the occupational health and safety criteria for the selection of contractors in the contractual documents.

Note: Coordination with external providers can assist an organization to address any impact outsourcing has on its OH&S performance.

Both notes are providing advice on how to address a requirement.

ISO 45001 Clause 9.1, "Monitoring Measurement Analysis and Performance Evaluation" and 10.2 "Incident, Non-conformity and Corrective Action"

Note: There can be legal requirements or other requirements that is national and international standards concerning the calibration or verification of monitoring and measuring equipment.

Note: The reporting and investigation of incidents without undue delay can enable hazards to be eliminated and associated OH&S risks to be minimized as soon as possible.

Both these notes provide information the organization or third-party auditor should discover somewhere other than in a management system standard.

ISO 45001 8.1.3, "Management of Change" and 6.1.3 "Determination of Legal Requirements and Other Requirements"

Note: Changes can result in risks and opportunities.

Note: Legal requirements and other requirements can result in risks and opportunities for the organization.

Both notes provide advice to the organization that assumes it doesn't understand that changes can create risks and that violating laws is risky.

The ISO 9001:2008 quality management standard, the ISO 14001:2004 environmental standard, and BS OHSAS 18001:2007 did not include the over-indexing, cross-referencing, and prescriptive notes found in the latest revisions: ISO 9001:2015, ISO 14001:2015 and ISO 45001:2018. Each of the older standards could have modified a few clauses to provide the addition of risk management and emphasis on management involvement, worker participation and procurement, and outsourcing controls. Annex SL provided more harm to the three standards with little helpful enhancements, in my opinion.

I would appreciate your feedback. You can contact me at dentchm@aol.com or visit my website at www.mpd-qe-consulting.com.

Appendix A
ISO 45001:2018 Definitions[2]

Audit: Systematic, independent, and documented process for obtaining audit evidence and evaluating it objectively to determine the extent to which the audit criteria are fulfilled.

Competence: Ability to apply knowledge and skills to achieve intended results.

Conformity: Fulfilment of a requirement.

Consultation: Seeking views before making a decision.

Continual improvement: Recurring activity to enhance performance.

Contractor: External organization providing services to the organization in accordance with agreed specifications, terms, and conditions.

Corrective action: Action to eliminate the cause(s) of a nonconformity or an incident and to prevent recurrence.

Documented information: Information required to be controlled and maintained by an organization and the medium on which it is contained.

Effectiveness: Extent to which planned activities are realized and planned results achieved.

Hazard: Source with a potential to cause injury and/or ill health.

Incident: Occurrence arising out of, or in the course of, work that could or does result in injury and/or ill health.

Injury and ill health: Adverse effect on the physical, mental, or cognitive condition of a person.

Legal requirements and other requirements: Legal requirements that an organization has to comply with and other requirements that an organization has to, or chooses to, comply with.

Management system: Set of interrelated or interacting elements of an organization that establishes policies and objectives and processes to achieve those objectives.

Measurement: Process to determine a value.

Monitoring: Determining the status of a system, a process, or an activity.

---

[2]   Source: ISO 45001:2018.

Nonconformity: Nonfulfilment of a requirement.

Objective: Result to be achieved.

Occupational health and safety management system: Management system or part of a management system used to achieve the OH&S policy.

Occupational health and safety opportunity: OH&S opportunity circumstance or set of circumstances that can lead to improvement of OH&S performance.

Occupational health and safety performance: OH&S performance related to the effectiveness of the prevention of injury and ill health to workers and the provision of safe and healthy workplaces.

Occupational health and safety policy: Policy to prevent work-related injury and ill health to workers and to provide a safe and healthy workplace.

Occupational health and safety risk: Combination of the likelihood of occurrence of a work-related hazardous event or exposure(s) and the severity of injury and ill health that can be caused by the event or exposure(s).

Organization: Person or group that has its own functions with responsibilities, authorities, and relationships to achieve its objectives.

Outsource: To make an arrangement where an external organization performs part of an organization's function or process.

Participation: Involvement in decision-making.

Performance: A measurable result.

Policy: Intentions and direction of an organization, as formally expressed by its top management.

Procedure: Specified way to carry out an activity or process.

Process: Set of interrelated or interacting activities that transform inputs into outputs.

Requirement: Need or expectation that is stated, generally implied, or obligatory.

Risk: Effect of uncertainty.

Top management: Person or group who directs and controls an organization at the highest level.

Worker: Person performing work or work-related activities that are under the control of the organization.

Workplace: Location under the control of the organization (3.1) where a person needs to be or to go for work purposes.

Appendix B
All About VPP

WHAT IS VPP?

The Voluntary Protection Programs (VPP) promotes effective worksite-based safety and health. In the VPP, management, labor, and OSHA establish cooperative relationships at workplaces that have implemented a comprehensive safety and health management system. Approval into VPP is OSHA's official recognition of the outstanding efforts of employers and employees who have achieved exemplary occupational safety and health.

WHAT IS THE AUTHORITY FOR VPP?

The legislative underpinning for VPP is Section (2)(b)(1) of the Occupational Safety and Health Act of 1970, which declares the Congress's intent "to assure so far as possible every working man and woman in the Nation safe and healthful working conditions and to preserve our human resources—by encouraging employers and employees in their efforts to reduce the number of occupational safety and health hazards at their places of employment, and to stimulate employers and employees to institute new and to perfect existing programs for providing safe and healthful working conditions."

HOW DOES VPP WORK?

In practice, VPP sets performance-based criteria for a managed safety and health system, invites sites to apply, and then assesses applicants against these criteria. OSHA's verification includes an application review and a rigorous onsite evaluation by a team of OSHA safety and health experts.

OSHA approves qualified sites to one of three programs:

Star: Recognition for employers and employees who demonstrate exemplary achievement in the prevention and control of occupational safety and health hazards, and the development, implementation, and continuous improvement of their safety and health management system

Merit: Recognition for employers and employees who have developed and implemented good safety and health management systems but who must take additional steps to reach Star quality.

Demonstration: Recognition for employers and employees who operate effective safety and health management systems that differ from current VPP requirements. This program enables OSHA to test the efficacy of different approaches.

WHEN DID VPP BEGIN?

1979: California began experimental program

1982: OSHA formally announced the VPP and approved the first site

1998: Federal worksites became eligible for VPP

HOW HAS VPP IMPROVED WORKER SAFETY & HEALTH?

Statistical evidence for VPP's success is impressive. The average VPP worksite has a Days Away Restricted or Transferred (DART) case rate of 52% below the average for its industry. These sites typically do not start out with such low rates. Reductions in injuries and illnesses begin when the site commits to the VPP approach to safety and health management and the challenging VPP application process.

HOW DOES VPP BENEFIT EMPLOYERS?

Fewer injuries and illnesses mean greater profits as workers' compensation premiums and other costs plummet. Entire industries benefit as VPP sites evolve into models of excellence and influence practices industry-wide.

HOW DOES VPP BENEFIT OSHA?

OSHA gains a corps of ambassadors enthusiastically spreading the message of safety and health system management. These partners also provide OSHA with valuable input and augment its limited resources.

Another benefit to OSHA is a safety and health advocacy group that came into existence as a result of the VPP, the Voluntary Protection Program Participants' Association (VPPPA). The VPPPA is a nonprofit organization founded in 1985. As part of its efforts to share the benefits of cooperative programs, the VPPPA works closely with OSHA and State Plan States in the development and implementation of cooperative programs. The VPPPA also provides expertise to these groups in the form of comments and stakeholder feedback on agency rulemaking and policies. Additionally, the Association provides comments and testimony to members of Congress regarding legislative bills on health and safety issues.

WHAT ARE SOME UNIQUE VPP INNOVATIONS?

Particularly noteworthy is the OSHA Special Government Employees Program (SGE) created in 1994. The SGE Program offers private and public sector safety and health professionals and other qualified participants the opportunity to exchange ideas, gain new perspectives, and grow professionally while serving as full-fledged team members on OSHA's VPP onsite evaluations.

If you are employed at a VPP site, see how you can help OSHA and VPP while gaining valuable experience!

Appendix C
Correspondence: ISO 45001:2018 to OHSAS 18001:2007

#	ISO 45001:2018	#	OHSAS 18001:2007
4	Context of the organization	4	OH&S management system requirements
4.1	Understanding the organization and its context	4.1	General requirements
4.2	Understanding needs and expectations of workers and other interested parties		NEW
4.3	Determining the scope of the OH&S management system	4.1	General requirements
4.4	OH&S management system	4.1	General requirements
5	Leadership and worker participation	4	Implementation and operation
5.1	Leadership and commitment	4.4.1	Resources, roles, responsibility, accountability, and authority
5.2	OH&S policy	4.2	OH&S policy
5.3	Organizational roles, responsibilities, and authorities	4.4.1	Resources, roles, responsibility, accountability, and authority
5.4	Consultation and participation of workers	4.4.3.2	Participation and consultation
6	Planning	4.3	Planning
6.1	Actions to address risks and opportunities		NEW
6.1.1	General		
6.1.2	Hazard identification and assessment of risks and opportunities	4.3.1	Hazard identification, risk assessment, and determining controls
6.1.3	Determination of legal requirements and other requirements	4.3.2	Legal and other requirements
6.1.4	Planning action		
6.2	Objectives and planning to achieve them		
6.2.1	OH&S objectives	4.3.3	Objectives and programme(s)
6.2.2	Planning to achieve OH&S objectives		NEW

#	ISO 45001:2018	#	OHSAS 18001:2007
7	Support		
7.1	Resources	4.4.1	Resources, roles, responsibility, accountability, and authority
7.2	Competence	4.4.2	Competence, training, and awareness
7.3	Awareness	4.4.2	Competence, training, and awareness
7.4	Communication		Communication, participation, and consultation
7.4.1	General	4.4.3.1	Communication
7.4.2	Internal communication	4.4.3.1	Communication
7.4.3	External communication	4.4.3.1	Communication
7.5	Documented information	4.4.4	Documentation
7.5.1	General	4.4.4	Documentation
7.5.2	Creating and updating		NEW
7.5.3	Control of documented information	4.4.4 4.5.4	Control of documents Control of records
8	Operation	4.4.6	Operational control
8.1	Operational planning and control	4.4	Implementation and operation (title only)
8.1.1	General		
8.1.2	Eliminating hazards and reducing OH&S risks	4.3.1	Hazard identification, risk assessment, and determining control
8.1.3	Management of change	4.3.1g, h	Hazard identification, risk assessment, and determining control
8.1.4	Procurement	4.3.1g, h	Hazard identification, risk assessment, and determining control
8.2	Emergency preparedness and response	4.4.6b	Operational control
9	Performance evaluation	4.5	Checking (title only)
9.1	Monitoring, measurement, analysis, and evaluation	4.5.1	Performance measurement and monitoring
9.1.1	General		
9.1.2	Evaluation of compliance	4.5.2	Evaluation of compliance
9.2	Internal audit	4.5.5	Internal audit
9.2.2	Internal audit program	4.5.5	Internal audit
9.3	Management review	4.6	Management review
10.1	General	4.1 4.2	General requirements OH&S policy

#	ISO 45001:2018	#	OHSAS 18001:2007
10.2	Nonconformity and corrective action	4.5.3	Incident investigation, nonconformity, corrective action, and preventive action (title only)
		4.5.3.1	Incident investigation
		4.5.3.2	Nonconformity, corrective and preventive action
10.3	Continual improvement	4.1	General requirements
		4.6	Management review

Index

Note: Page numbers followed by *f* or *t* refer to figures or tables, respectively.

NOTES

NOTES

NOTES

NOTES

NOTES

NOTES

www.ingramcontent.com/pod-product-compliance
Lightning Source LLC
Chambersburg PA
CBHW081109220326
41598CB00038B/7282